FATHER, SON & THE UNHOLY ROAD

Scripture quotations marked ESV are taken from the English Standard Version of the Bible.
Scripture quotations marked LSB are taken from the Legacy Standard Bible New Testament with Psalms and Proverbs

Cover Art: Penelope Jane
Cover Design: Brad Henderson
Back Cover Photograph: Jason Myers

ISBN 978-0-578-85850-0 (hardcover and paperback)
ISBN 978-0-578-85852-4 (digital)

Distributed to the general market trade by Ingram Publishing

Printed in the United States of America

email: lanny@TippingPT.coach
website: www.tippingpt.coach

FATHER, SON & THE UNHOLY ROAD

The Dark, Twisted Truth About My Journey From Cocaine To Christ

Lanny West

with Chris Parton

TPEG, llc

Lanny and Brother Fred Wolfe
(November 2020)
Photo by: Don Davis

In Loving Memory of Brother Fred Wolfe
Thank you for your spiritual mentorship, for staying true to God's Word, your love and your unwavering encouragement. I am a better disciple and man because of you.

This book is dedicated to the father I never knew
and to the Father that has always known me.

And to all those who have bitten the forbidden fruit
and feel there is no hope and no way out.
I pray that this book will help you discover the gift of
our Father's loving grace and forgiveness!

My Birth Father
Photographer:
Unknown

*"I believe there is no limit to what a man can do
if he doesn't care who gets the credit for it!"*
Lt. Col. Donald E. Downard, CO,
2d Battalion, 222d Regiment

Lanny & Leslie
Photo by: Nan Fisher

So I am often asked.... How have you managed to make this marriage last for over 29 years? 1st) You must be BEST FRIENDS, 2nd) BE KNITTED TOGETHER AS ONE, 3rd) ENJOY BEING LOVERS, 4th) COMPROMISE ALWAYS, 5th) CORRECT WITH LOVE, 6th) BE ENCOURAGING, 7th) BE HUSBAND AND WIFE and 8) UNDERSTAND THAT THERE IS NO PERFECT RELATION-SHIP. WE ARE IMPERFECT BEINGS..... IT TAKES WORK AND GUIDANCE FROM GOD. There are a few other little secrets but best left for another time. Those many years ago I joined life forces with THE MOST amazing woman on the planet. She took this broken man into her life and her heart with no questions asked........ well maybe "Can you cook". She is a guiding light on life's perilous journey. If the measure of success in one's life is evaluated by only one human endeavor ...... I did it on May 1, 1992! Leslie, I love you more today than yesterday but not as much as tomorrow.

SPECIAL THANKS

Don Davis - Thank you for your love, your strength, your steadfast biblical mentorship, for never giving up on me, and for baptizing me in my hot tub. You are truly my John The Baptist!

Chris Parton - Thank you for bringing life to my words and story. It has been a very special experience working with you on this project!

Cliff Shiepe - Thank you for your encouragement, guidance and love!

Richard Tyre - Thank you for believing in me, for your undying friendship and for allowing me to stretch my creative wings.

Wiley Post - Thank you for your continued friendship and for believing in me all those many years ago. Without your support my radio career might never have blossomed.

Marty Winsch - Thank you for your unfailing and continued friendship, partnerships and mentorship. Never in all my years have I felt strong enough about someone to call them Best Friend..... until our paths collided. Dreaming big and your partnership in many great adventures is unparalleled!

CONTENTS

CONTENTS

FORWARD

by **MARTY WINSCH**

My cameo here is nothing compared to the floor seats I was given to this story, a rare non-obstructed view that only starts around Chapter 20. It was toward the end of the tale, and mostly allowed due to my regular attendance itself – it kept my membership from expiring – but it left a mark on me all the same.

You see, the phone call I received from Lanny in 1996 changed my life. Some calls are like that, and you can usually tell. Mine was exciting at the time in a purely self-serving sense. But what I didn't realize was I'd just received my first phone call from my best friend. To say now that I'm happy to be standing here on this page would be true, and it is true, except for the horror I feel over the weight of responsibility to, as they say, get it right. So, if there's such a thing as needlessly bludgeoning words to death, either physically or emotionally, consider your visual of me to be jumping up and down with joy. I'm happy to be found guilty as charged.

At this very moment I am struggling to not detest this task, trying as I might to place into such a tiny frame a perfect articulation of a miracle. A man who, for the benefit of everyone in his life, yielded to the idea of loving himself as the cornerstone to fulfilling his personal calling by God. What I can say about this story with utmost certainty, though, is that the war Lanny wages against time is very serious and very real, and each tick and tock leads him closer to a revelation: That his journey is absolute evidence of the Glory of God ... it was hiding in plain sight all along.

Is there a better story ever told than that? I think not.

And like two old men in their waning years, sparring now with board games rather than boxing gloves, I visualize my dear friend walking straight into the trap I've laid here, filled as it is with love and acknowledgement. He would undoubtedly deflect any credit and accuse me of overindulgence and blasphemy. At which point I would ask "Have you ever heard the one about the once hollowed-shell of a man, who was humbled by his own transformation? The man who now stands with absolute purpose and clear eyes, gazing out over the glorious hills of a small Tennessee farm to keep a watchful eye on his soul, and all the others that have been trusted upon him?" He'd say "No." But read on and you will.

Introduction

With arrogance comes only quarreling, But with those who receive counsel is wisdom.
Proverbs 13:10 (LSB)

I was dead. I was dead in my trespasses and sinking in the quagmire of my own sins. As hard as I tried, I was just unable to change my life. I did not want to know God. I did not love God. I had no reason to trust God. I found God boring, and quite frankly, I did not want God around. Therefore, I was a slave to my own sin. And that is the condition of everyone ... until God moves.

It felt like I was waking up from a dream. That sense of being suddenly alert, when you're not quite sure if your last memory can be trusted. But as I was slowly realizing, this was all too real.

I blinked the dryness from my eyes and shook my head, completely disoriented as I drifted back from something close to an out-of-body experience. And as my vision refocused, I looked around and remembered where I was. Nope, I wasn't just waking up.

An auditorium full of blank faces stared back at me—some with their mouths open in disbelief, others just perplexed. You could hear a pin drop and my blood ran ice cold. As I looked left and looked right, I saw my peers with that same confused look.

Oh no, I thought to myself in a panic. What did I just do? Did I say something I shouldn't have?

It was starting to come back to me. I was on stage at the WME talent agency in Nashville as part of an expert panel for the Music Health Alliance, asked to discuss mental health issues in the music industry. Speaking engagements aren't really my thing, but I'd been on a few panels like this over the years, and agreed to do it for a friend. I had just gotten my degree as a wellness and lifestyle coach, and also had decades of experience in radio, the club business, and management, so my friend thought I'd be perfect for the panel. So far he'd been right.

I spoke about the power of adding magnesium supplements to your diet, and weighed in on dealing with adversity of all kinds. I was happy to share my thoughts and expertise if it would help someone, and the whole thing was shaping up to be a soft-ball Q&A session. I was on cruise control, just coasting through until the after-hours festivities started later on. Everything seemed fine.

Somebody had raised their hand and asked a normal enough question—something about how childhood trauma could affect one's ability to be successful in business. Someone else on the panel kicked off the answering, but then the ball was tossed to me. And as I started giving my opinion, a whole tangle of long-buried trauma began pouring out.

Things I hadn't thought about in sixty years . . . things I had purposely never told a single soul. Things I had blocked out of my memory entirely. I had just spilled my guts out on the floor in front of all these people, and judging by their reaction, it was pretty gruesome.

I shared the fact that, as a child, I had been sexually assaulted by another boy, and I had never told anyone until now. It was a strange place to make a breakthrough, but I didn't even really know I was doing it. It was like I blacked out and just unloaded all this weight from my soul.

Come to think of it, it actually felt pretty good. I had never experienced what it was like to have an unburdened soul. I suddenly realized I had always felt crushed by my past. And although I had never given it any thought, for the first time in my life I think I felt the presence of God. He was trying to tell me something.

I walked off that stage feeling a thousand times lighter than I had before, completely oblivious to the whispers and weird looks that followed me. And from that moment on something changed. I went home feeling like there was something I needed to do. Some bones I needed to dig up from the past. But it would still be a while before I could truly do it. That time has finally come.

For many years I've shared with friends the crazy, unbelievable stories that stitch my life together, starting as a kid and running through careers in radio, entertainment, and artist management—plus about fifteen lifetimes worth of romantic drama.

Without fail, those who heard the stories encouraged me to write a book like this, sharing the way I lived in good times and bad. But until now I laughed the idea off. It would just be a collection of XXX-rated stories with no redeeming value or pay-off—and most likely leave readers blushing, if not horrified.

Just a few years out of high school I was a high-flying DJ and Music Director at the beginning of FM radio's explosion. I ran infamous nightclubs and navigated the seedy underbelly of the live entertainment world. I booked and promoted massive rock concerts with ZZ Top, Leon Russell, Molly Hatchet, and more, served as the general manager of a national music magazine, opened three retail clothing stores, developed a new restaurant concept, and transitioned into full-on artist management—all while doing enough blow to earn a rewards card from Scarface's Tony Montana.

Back then I really lived the sex, drugs, and rock 'n' roll lifestyle. I did whatever I wanted, whenever I wanted (sometimes barely living to tell the tale), and the whole time I acted like I somehow had backstage access to the inner workings of the universe. But, in fact, the opposite was true. I was a stranger to myself and often a danger to others, rocketing from one bed, one relationship, one career to the next.

To be honest, I didn't write the book earlier because of questions like, "What could I share that would actually help?" and "Who would really give a shit?" But I'm in a different place now. The past four years have exposed the payoff I needed and given me the tools to sit down and start sharing, and I intend to share every gritty detail.

I'm ready to take you on a wild journey that ends on a hopeful note—a sixty-five-plus-year trip of emotional and physical abuse, six marriages, five divorces, success, disappointment, sexual addiction, substance abuse, alcohol, near-death experience, murderous rage, accidentally partnering with a real-life crime boss, payola (aka pay for play), perversion, and many years in a business notorious for its shady underside. Some of it was happy, some was reckless, and some was just plain outrageous, but it all led to three pivotal moments.

First, when I married my best friend and soul mate in the early 1990s. Second, when I finally quit my fifty-plus year career in entertainment to discover who I really was. And third, how I ended up owning forty acres of spiritual farm land, accepting Jesus Christ, and being baptized in a hot tub.

Why write this book? Simply put, it was time. Actually long overdue. But I could not share the story until God was ready and had finished His work.

This book is my life story. It's about love and the lack of it, success and monumental failure, music, family, and the self-destructive nature of man. It's a book about sex, drugs, anger, and ambition. It's about the best advice I ever got, and it may shock you. It may make you mad. But you may also recognize a sliver of yourself in it. You'll understand the hunger in my soul for a feeling of connection, and see that everything I did was subconsciously intended to satisfy that.

I have a lot to share, but I don't mean to glorify the madness. This is a cautionary tale and a lifeline for those who feel far from God. A modern-day version of Jesus' Parable of the Prodigal Son, and my hope is that someone out there benefits from it.

We all need to feel like we have a place in the world, a home where we belong and are loved unconditionally. We'll even make one of our own if we have to, and mine was a pretty legendary house of sin. But right there onstage at the WME panel, I realized I was actually trapped in that house I had built—and I had no idea how to get out.

This book is for anyone who has found themselves trapped like that, and especially for those who are still wondering how they'll get out and heal the broken pieces of their life. What I discovered was that another house existed. A healthy house, custom built for each of us. And to find it, all I had to do was listen.

Part 1

The Sound of Silence

For I know the plans I have for you, declares the LORD, plans for welfare and not for evil, to give you a future and a hope.

Jeremiah 29: 11 (ESV)

1

Please Allow Me To Introduce Myself

This story starts in the dark, with a clever but quirky young teenager sitting alone by the window each night, long after he was supposedly in bed. I remember spending hours like that, staring out into nothing and turning the dial on my little transistor radio as I waited for sleep.

Back then, I was just hoping to catch a signal from Nashville—or maybe even Chicago on a lucky night—hoping beyond hope to hear the sounds of a far-away city filled with music and adventure. But I know now I was really searching for something different.

Back then, I didn't know one single thing about my father. And up until recently, I had only seen a few faded black-and-white pictures of him. Even those were hard to come by since he and my mother were long divorced.

Actually, scratch that. I knew one thing of Lt. Colonel Donald Ephraim Downard—that he was a bad guy and that I should not be like him. It was drilled into me and my brother, David, like a jukebox on repeat, a daily reminder that I came from spoiled stock. But in the end, not being like him was easier said than done.

I was born in 1952 on an Army base in what was then Elizabeth City County, Virginia—but my name was not Lanny West. It was a chaotic time in the American South, as an earthquake of social change began to ripple in waves across the land, and in that respect, Boyd Anthony Downard fit right in. Right from the beginning, chaos seemed to rule over every aspect of my life.

In the little western Georgia towns where I grew up, things were still done the old way. Each one had a mill and a drug store and a movie theater—they were basically all Mayberry from The Andy Griffith Show—and desegregation was only just beginning to roll back Jim Crow. Almost every town was surrounded by farmland and had a little square in the middle with a courthouse and a church. The boys either played football and baseball or got picked on by those who did (that was me), and the girls wore skirts and ribbons in their hair and led cheers for the varsity teams.

Everybody knew where the make-out spot was—even the cops—and there always seemed to be a family of bootleggers just outside town with five or six refrigerators on the back deck full of hooch for sale, provided you had the nerve to show up there. Life was slow and steady and parents had certain expectations of their children—not the other way around. But it was obviously all changing. By the end, I would take it upon myself to test the limits in a thousand ways.

Like I said, my father was nowhere to be found, because according to my mother, she caught him in bed with a local girl while we were stationed in Japan and filed for divorce. She wasn't raised to accommodate such things apparently—especially if they happened more than once. And as far as I could tell, she never looked back or wondered what might have been, even though it left her in a bad spot. I think I was two, and at the time, she was pregnant with David. So he and I were raised by my mother and a pair of dysfunctional stepfathers.

Mother was born Antonia Martha Weiniger in Graz, Austria, and came to the United States after meeting my father overseas. She had hoped to become a model and was forced to give up the dream when I was born, but still kept a claw-like grip on her vision of a glitzy, high-society lifestyle. So once she left my father, her quest for a suitable husband commenced.

She was authoritarian in every sense of the word, ruling over David and me through the haze of two packs a day and a wardrobe that was never, ever out of style. I'm not sure how she pulled that off, honestly, but it had a lot to do with the guys she ended up with. They needed deep pockets, not big hearts.

The wooden spoon and the leather belt were our nemeses, and she wielded them with cruel abandon at seemingly random times, often punishing the smallest infraction with the same intensity as a major violation of "order." She showed us no love, that's for sure. But she also played us German operas, taught me to cook, and made sure I had the opportunity to learn piano and as many instruments as the school band offered to teach. She wasn't evil, but she cared mostly for her own comfort and social standing. And she always ended up drawn to men just like my father.

First up was Bass Lewis, a lawyer in Columbus, Georgia, who's appetite for an African safari was only matched by a thirst for booze. We lived on Habersham Avenue, and being so young, I don't remember much. But I do know we were close with Bass's wealthy cousin Bobby and Bobby's wife, Jean. That was a plus for my mother, I think. She wanted the luxurious life they lived, and being their friend let her pretend she had it. The validation was priceless in her eyes, and worth a lot of grief. But after a few years, it all went to hell. Her marriage with Bass went up in a ball of flames so hot I think it singed me forever, and looking back now, it's amazing I didn't wind up in prison.

One of my earliest memories is of Columbus getting its first McDonald's. That was a big deal back then, especially in a small city. Obviously, the family had to go out for dinner and try this all-American phenomenon, and I remember being so proud of myself for eating two twenty-five cent hamburgers. I couldn't wait to go back.

Then, on the way home, Bass almost killed us.

We all knew he was exceptionally drunk that day, and on the drive home, he was speeding like a bat out of hell—way too fast for the curvy, two-lane road we were on. Something had to give. David and I were in the back with no seatbelts on, and after a few miles, I could just tell Bass was no longer paying attention.

Telephone poles whipped by as the engine howled, and as we approached a big, ninety-degree turn, I could see my mother tense up slightly. Her lips had barely parted to scream as Bass swung the wheel left at the last second, and with two wheels in the air like one of those traveling stunt shows, we were all flung to the right side of the car.

I lost my center of gravity for what seemed like an eternity, the car still hurtling and now skidding through gravel on the edge of the road. Stones pelted the fenders as the ground got closer and closer to the window, but somehow, Bass got it back on four wheels.

The car slammed into the ground and tossed us back to the left, and as soon as we leveled out, my mother was hollering and hitting and cursing at Bass—understandably so. But in that same instant, Bass transitioned from an oblivious drunk into a blind rage, cursing back at her and waving his fist while gunning the engine once more.

I honestly don't remember getting home, but somehow we ended up back in the driveway with my mother still screaming. Bass had had enough. He reached under the seat and fished out a shiny silver revolver, and then just looked at her, wild-eyed, with his fingers wrapped around the grip in a white-knuckled squeeze. And slowly, he leveled that pistol right at her head.

A long moment ticked by, and then another. But my mother didn't hesitate.

2

A Pattern In The Static

The car was still running after our near wreck, and Bass was still fuming and pointing the gun in my mother's face. But when she made her move, she called his bluff with a level of courage I can still hardly comprehend.

She ripped us out of the car and dragged us through the house into my bedroom, pulling the telephone in behind us and slamming the door. Meanwhile, Bass continued to scream and rave, and I caught a glimpse of him waving the gun as we collapsed to the floor. I held David's hand while my mother fumbled with the phone, trying desperately to call Aunt Jean and fighting back the fear that made her hands tremble.

Luckily, Jean picked up. She must have seen this coming because she instantly understood my mother's frantic sobs, and it didn't take long for her to get to the house. We climbed out the bedroom window and sprinted to her car, with Bass still beating on the door to get in.

I'm sure now that he was too drunk to follow through with whatever blackness was in his head, but it was frightening to say the least. Jean took us to the Lewis family farm where we stayed until the dust settled, and I don't remember my mother and Bass ever seeing each other again. It was over.

To be honest, I can't say I really understood what had happened—I was too young. But on another level, what reason did I have to assume this wasn't how every relationship ended?

———————

We stayed close with Aunt Jean. And it wasn't long before she helped my mother find another husband.

George Patterson was in medical school doing a residency in Columbus. And although he wasn't a drunk or violent man, he also wasn't an emotional kind of guy—to put it lightly. He was very straightforward, and I never remember seeing any kind of love between the two of them. But his patients thought the sun rose and set on this guy.

George was a good doctor. There's no question about that, but at home he was a miserable sack of unhappiness. He doted on his kids, but showed no love to me and David. He was impossible to crack.. My mother was still only interested in her social calendar, especially now that she was relieved of the need to find David and I another "father."

We moved to Cuthbert, Georgia, where George joined a medical group. But he quit after falling out with his partners and opened his own practice in the huge old house we lived in. It had been a hospital during the Civil War, and after my half-brother Mark was born, we instantly had a big, blended family of five boys, since George had two sons from a previous marriage, George Jr. and Bobby.

In little towns like Cuthbert, the doctor was always on call, and I distinctly remember people showing up at the house at all hours. We were having dinner one Sunday and there was a knock at the back door, so I got up and answered it. There in the threshold stood a young woman with a bullet hole in her chest, bleeding everywhere. She had been a patient of George's at one point, I guess, so without so much as an "excuse me," he took her back and removed the bullet. Meanwhile, dinner just carried on.

Apparently, this woman had gotten into an argument with her girl-friend over a pack of chewing gum, and I'm still surprised she survived. But the crazy thing is, this sort of thing didn't even phase me, which is maybe saying something.

There were other things to be traumatized by—like church.

We lived right across the street from the town's Methodist church, and despite the fact that neither parent had a religious bone in their body, mother wanted us to go for the sake of appearances. Even though I was only about eight years old, this bothered me to no end. It wasn't that the preacher dragged on and on about ancient stories, or that we were kicked out of the first pew we chose because one of the town's more "established" families normally sat there. It wasn't even that the whole event was clearly a fashion show, which my mother dove into headfirst. It was the fact I had never seen a Bible in my entire life, and I knew we had no intention of bringing any of this back to the house across the street. It was all just pretend in my eyes, and I held on to that belief for a very long time.

Meanwhile, I was finding ways to traumatize myself.

I already understood that my parents were different than most families. They just didn't care. Kids like us were an obligation, and love was just a word in storybooks. By now I was playing piano, coronet, trumpet, baritone, tuba, and more, but never in my entire childhood did George show up to one of my band recitals—not even later when I started play-ing for the cheerleaders at football games. He always seemed to look through me.

I remember trying over and over to win his affection by connecting to something he enjoyed—subconsciously trying to score myself a male role model, I guess—but he didn't enjoy anything except work. I was my mother's "problem" in his eyes, and she was not much of a problem solver. They stayed about as absent as possible while physically being present, so I stayed gone from the house as much as I could, and this led to some scary moments.

When I was thirteen, a neighborhood friend and I got interested in Molotov cocktails, probably because it was 1965 and the Watts riots had just burned an entire section of Los Angeles. We figured out how to make a Molotov of our own (it wasn't hard). And I can't tell you what possessed me to do this, but I decided to make a little mayhem. The backyard of our house was fenced in and basically a parking lot, but right in the corner of the fence was a little opening, just big enough for a skinny kid like me to squeeze through. On the other side was our neighbor's house with a barn out back, and that's where I decided my dastardly deed would take place.

What you're supposed to do with a Molotov is light the rag you've stuffed in the gasoline-filled Coke bottle, and then throw it, letting the bottle hit something and explode into a ball of fire. But what I did was set the bottle at the corner of the barn and light the rag. Then I ran like hell.

I sprinted to the other end of the barn and around a corner where I could look back at the burning bottle, and all of a sudden something inside me said, "You've screwed up."

Panicking, I ran back over, picked up some sticks and started throwing them at the bottle, thinking if I knocked it over the rag would go out. That didn't work. Instead, it just knocked the bottle over and made a big puddle of fire, so I freaked out and went over to stomp out the growing flames. I was fortunate it didn't explode . . . but I did get gas all over my pants. And it caught them on fire, big time.

With flames climbing up my legs, I ran down the side of the barn to the barbed wire fence. I jumped over the fence before it finally occurred to me to roll around on the ground. I tried and tried to roll the flames out, feeling the heat and smelling the stink of burning flesh, but I was wearing polyester corduroys (which were basically made of oil even without the gas) and I couldn't get the fire out. I was officially freaking out, and the only thing I can imagine now is that God intervened. I suddenly realized the only way to fix this was to stand up while I was on fire, undo my belt, pull my pants down, and smother the whole thing.

I was in shock, and I had third-degree burns on both legs from my ankles to my knees. I limped back to the house blubbering and scared as the pain began to take hold. Finally, mercifully, I ran into Betty, the housekeeper who worked for us and would later teach me to drive. She took me to George who, for once, showed some compassion, and took me to his office at the back of the house.

By this time, it was clear my legs had been burned down to the bone. You could see muscle, and it got to the point that I couldn't walk because the skin and muscle were so contracted. But George cleaned up both of the wounds, bandaged me, and took me to the bedroom, where he immediately gave me morphine. In the meantime, the barn burned down, and since his office was right next door, the fire chief came by wanting to know if George had treated anybody for burns. Even more shocking than the fire, my stepfather continued to show compassion for me, and lied. He said he had not seen anyone, and I guess I would have been in a whole lot of trouble if he had told the truth.

I was out of school for a month and confined to bed, covered in skin grafts taken from my right thigh. Later on, I was embarrassed and wouldn't wear shorts because of the scars, but the only thing I can say is that God had no intention of me dying that day at the barn. I still don't like being around fire, but I learned a lot from this episode. Maybe most of all, I learned I needed to literally be on fire for this man to care for me.

Despite my home life, Cuthbert wasn't all bad. I began listening to the radio show hosted by John Ron Nashville's WLAC and discovered an escape in music that would last a lifetime. I had thoughts and feelings I just couldn't talk about with my parents, but somehow guys like Otis Redding and even Elvis seemed to get me.

During that time, I have vivid memories of watching The Beatles' American debut on our black-and-white TV in Cuthbert. I also got my first job pumping gas at a neighborhood filling station (promptly losing it after misplacing some guy's gas cap) and kissed my first girl (Kay from down the street. I would invite her over to play touch football—a sly devil from the start). Those were good times, but I also got picked on mercilessly at school and only had a few friends, so when George got another job and we moved to West Point, Georgia, I didn't care.

West Point was yet another little town on the state border, straddling the Chattahoochee River and just a stone's throw from Lanett, Alabama. And by now I was a full-blown teenager, so my attention had turned in a predictable direction.

3

The Formative Years

For years, my mother, in her unending quest of social climbing, hosted parties at the family home using the three youngest boys as "butlers." I must admit, it was cute. We'd wear black suits and stand attentively against the wall, waiting to clear out glasses and hors d'oeuvres plates while guests clucked and preened and strutted around in too-expensive formal wear. To this day, I can still set a table that would make Emily Post proud because of those parties.

As I got older I realized what a gold mine the parties really were. Dozens of guests were invited each time, which meant the back pantry was stocked to the brim with liquor and mixers of all kinds. First, my brothers and I would experiment with whatever was in the glasses we brought back to the kitchen—a little champagne here, a little bourbon there. We'd get silly but never drunk and no one seemed to notice, so we kept pushing our luck.

Eventually, it got to the point where my friend John and I hatched a plan. He lived in the house that backed up to ours, and we were birds of a feather, so to speak, looking to stay gone from home as much as possible and prove our obvious (to us) coolness. There was a teen club in the basement beneath the school gym, only open to kids aged thirteen to seventeen, and good times could be had with the girls there—especially if we could bring them a gift.

Over the years, I saw bands like The Box Tops, Joe Cocker, and The Bushmen at that club, so it was always a popular hang. And now I had a plan. I told John there was a party coming up and I could get us a bottle fresh from the stash. My parents would never miss it, so on a soggy Friday night, I put the plot in motion.

With my brothers in the dark just as much as anyone else, we played our usual roles, gathering dishes and obliging the wrinkled old-timers with a ridiculous bow every now and again. But as the party wound down, I kept an eye on mother and George, who was skulking around like a low-rent James Bond. As soon as they went upstairs, I hustled into the pantry, opened up the liquor cabinet, grabbed the nearest bottle, and bolted out the front door.

As the screen slammed shut behind me, I knew it would be my hide if I got caught, so there was no time to waste. I booked it down the hill to meet John in our shadowy rendezvous spot. He was where he was supposed to be, so we climbed up on the train trestle and slipped across the river to relative safely—but not before narrowly missing an oncoming train.

With my master plan a resounding success, it was finally time to get teenage-drunk, and I turned to John with a smile only spies like us could share. With a whoop of triumph I reached into my bag and held that bottle up like a trophy. It was only then that I looked at the label . . . I had stolen a bottle of really dry sherry. It tasted like shit. But we drank it anyway.

From then on, John and I drank whenever we got the chance. He had a car so we'd ride out to the bootlegger's house and spend the money we made gathering pecans and mowing lawns. I quickly found out that when I was drinking, I had a different personality. I was cool and careless like Mick Jagger, and could dance with the wild abandon of Elvis. I liked it. And the friends we were hanging around seemed to like it too. More than they normally liked me anyway.

We'd go to parties and I wouldn't even want to drink a whole lot, but it felt like I had to, so I figured a workaround. We would get these tall-boy beers and go over to somebody's house when their parents weren't home. I would get a beer, sip on it for a while, then head to the bathroom. But while I was in there, I would pour the beer out, come back, and grab another. After several trips to the bathroom, it would seem like I was drinking a lot, which was exactly my plan, but really, I just wanted to fit in with the guys who could drink themselves unconscious. Every kid goes though something like that, but without a dad to help me understand my place in the world, I began to base a lot of my identity on partying. And anybody who's seen an episode of Behind the Music knows that's bad news.

It wasn't long before trying to have sex was an even bigger thrill than getting drunk, and in all honesty, it would become a bigger problem in my life than drugs or alcohol combined. I just didn't have a healthy sense of what it was all about or a single role model for loving relationships. So my warped view on sex started from the very beginning.

One of my earliest experiences was actually being assaulted by an older boy, and this is the story that came pouring out of me on the WME stage. His family was friendly with mine so we went to their house for dinner sometimes, and no matter what, we always got sent away to play by ourselves in his room. And that's where it happened.

I was young and easily manipulated, I guess, and he was always talking about sex and how it was done. But I never really thought anything of it. He was just kind of weird as far as I was concerned. But that eventually turned into him exposing himself to me, and then one night, right after dinner, he bent me over his bed and started penetrating me anally.

It really happened that fast—so fast I had no idea what was going on—and it hurt like absolute hell. But I was too scared and ashamed to tell my parents. Maybe if we had been closer, I would have gotten some help, but instead, I think I tried to erase the incident from my memory. I didn't want to get in trouble, I didn't want to be bad like my father, so I just wouldn't let myself feel the trauma. Not exactly a healthy response, but it worked for me . . . and it became my approach for just about everything.

That terrible moment didn't return to my thoughts until much later in life—about fifty years later and in front of a bunch of strangers. And perhaps that's a blessing, but I do think now, it set the stage for the messed up way I viewed sex. From then on, that moment was like a record skipping in the back of my mind, secretly replaying over and over.

Most of the time I barely registered on my stepfather George's radar, and that was on purpose. But one of the few really nice things he ever did for me (aside from the barn-burning incident) was buy me my first car. It was a 1962 Volkswagen Beetle in Rustoleum Red, and it became the setting for my first time. I knew a girl from Lanett who was known for being open to dating, and to my surprise, she said yes when I asked her to a drive-in movie.

I washed and cleaned that Beetle for a whole day, getting everything just right, and after proudly picking her up, things got steamy. We didn't even stay until the end of the movie, and instead left early to head out to the local parking spot. I was about to score my first hit.

It was an interesting evening, and let me just say you can have sex (or what I thought was sex) in the front seat of a Beetle. Where there's a will, there's a way. But it didn't turn out like I imagined, and the relationship only lasted a little while. Instead, my real first love was a girl named Dale, and she would ultimately become the first of my six wives.

Dale and I had known each other for years, but other than a small mutual crush, there was nothing between us. Her dad was the school principal and also the head football coach. One night after an out-of-town game we got the news that his wife (Dale's mom) was missing. It was devastating and crazy and Dale instantly became very distraught, and that's how our relationship began.

It was well known in town that Coach Lewis was a heavy drinker and the relationship between he and his wife was not the greatest, but he was obviously devastated. About four weeks after her disappearance—after I had been consoling Dale and having quite a lot of conversations—some county workers made a gruesome discovery.

They were trimming grass on Interstate 85 and saw something shiny near the bank of the Chattahoochee, and it turned out to be Dale's mom's car. She was in it, and they thought what happened was she had been drinking and somehow ran off the road (or was forced off of it). The car went off the interstate and landed pristinely between a pair of bridge abutments, dug out a whole scoop of earth and plopped down sideways in the river, in just such a way that you couldn't see it. It was terrible.

Sometimes, when emotional things happen, people have sex. It's a cliché, I know, and you see it all over in movies and TV. But it really was the case for Dale and me. We went out and I just wanted to comfort her, to help get rid of the loneliness I secretly felt in my own life, but we ended up in bed.

I don't know why, probably because there were all these negative associations connecting the sex to her trauma and mine, but it quickly got unhealthy. I got obsessed with things like telling her how to put on makeup and how to dress, then became jealously protective of her, wanting to make sure she didn't draw too much attention from other boys. Maybe I was trying to form her into what I envisioned a girl should be. But I had total control, so it went straight to the point where we were having sex all the time, always on my terms.

Almost every night I would go over to Dale's house for a visit (anything to not be at my house), and because I was great chums with her dad, he had no problem with it. He would drink himself into a stupor every night, so we'd wait until he was asleep and we could hear him snoring, get to it on the sofa, and then I'd go home.

It was a true experimental, "anything goes" kind of sexual adventure, and it would only be the first of many for me. We'd break up and get back together, break up and get back together what seemed like a thousand times, and sex was always in the makeup.

Looking back, it was the first proof of something that would plague me for most of the rest of my life—basically, that I had no idea how to love. I never saw the true love of a mother to a son, or learned how to show love from the guys my mother married, so I just had to wing it. The sex I was having was only the physical part of a relationship, and most of the time after the physical part was over, I didn't want anything else to do with them. But as long as they would give it up, I would hang out.

Where it ended up going was me figuring out that by marrying a girl, you could have sex with her anytime you wanted to. And if you got bored, you just got divorced and married another one.

I didn't know what was supposed to happen, all I knew was my mother was married several times to either a drunk, an abuser, or an emotionless human being. It was like a puzzle I was trying to put together, and some pieces came from this box, some from this other box. I wanted to fit them together, but I had no chance from the start. Plus, I was acting tough and not confronting my own fears of abandonment, and it all spelled trouble for the future.

But I didn't know any of this at the time. Instead, I just enjoyed the feeling of having sex and the control that came with it. And I also found my calling.

4

Face The Music

By high school, I was already living a pretty wild life compared to other kids, having regular sex and drinking whenever I wanted. But despite that, I was still a total nerd. Even today, I don't have many guy friends, and I think I've always been that way to avoid getting disappointed if they leave me behind, like my dad did. Even so, I craved connection and did become buddies with one of the "cool kids" back then—a senior named Alan who worked at the local radio station, WRLD. He knew I was into music and would let me sit in with him on Saturdays to empty the trash and file records . . . but also a little more.

If Alan made an announcement or got a record started, he let me sit in the seat and showed me how to segue to the next record and turn the knobs, and eventually all he had to do was come back over to play any commercials that had tags at the end. For instance, the drive-in movie theater might have a generic commercial, but there would be a card taped to it. You would flip it up and come on at the end to announce things like, "Tonight, You Only Live Twice is playing at 7 p.m."

I immediately loved being at the station—it was like I had found a new home. First of all, I loved listening to the music (you can get paid for that?). And second, there was a bit of stardom attached to it, and I was secretly harboring red-carpet dreams.

Near graduation, Alan and his friends had a grad party on a Friday night, and when I came in that Saturday morning, he was still drunk.

He hadn't even been to sleep yet, and honestly, I felt bad for the guy. He was throwing up in between records.

I got down to my usual business, doing segues and loading records, that kind of thing. And then it was time for a commercial—one with a tag at the end. I started it and said, "Alan, you need to come read a tag." But he goes, "Dude, I can't do it. I'm gonna go throw up. You do it."

I was shocked and excited and terrified all at the same time, and waiting to read that live tag was the longest sixty seconds of my entire life. The commercial ended, and I flipped the switch to read the tag—and I was hooked. When Alan left for college, I took his job.

Soon, I was either at the station or with Dale, and sometimes both. Dale would come hang out, and we would have sex while a record played. Then I would get back on the mic. But while I was there, the general manager tried to give me a radio name that was just not happening. Up until then, I was just Boyd, and this knucklehead thought it would be cool for me to be "Boppin' Boyd."

Can you imagine a kid who's already a nerd and getting bullied every day at school, doing a radio show with the name "Boppin' Boyd?" Not just "No," but "HELL NO!"

This happened to be the summer after Alan's graduation, and I was spending a few weeks at a YMCA camp with Alan continuing his radio show until college started in the fall. The camp was just outside Montgomery, Alabama, in Wetumpka on Lake Jordan, and one day we took a little road trip that was right up my alley. We went to tour a radio station I listened to all the time at camp: Montgomery's WHHY.

A DJ named Monte Parker was working when we arrived, and of course, I wanted to know everything about that station—but especially how Monte got his name. So I asked him. Nice as he was, he said, "Well,

Parker is my real last name. But Monte is short for Montgomery," and the lights went off in my little brain.

When I got back to my radio station, I realized its legal, top-of-the-hour ID was "WRLD, 1490 since 1940, Lanett, Alabama/West Point, Georgia." So, Lanny is short for Lanett, and West is short for West Point. I became Lanny West overnight.

But as good as things were going at work, I was still having trouble at home. My parents and I just could not connect on anything, and every once in a while, my mother would remind me that I was, in fact, just like my father. She would warn me to shape up by feeding me bits of info like the fact that he was a respected soldier in World War II, but had thrown it all away by getting court-martialed for writing bad checks, committing spousal abuse, and drinking too much. Eventually, I started wondering if she was right. Maybe I was just like him.

At one point, I needed new glasses and influenced by my new radio job, I picked out a pair of round frames just like John Lennon wore. Somehow, this threw George into a rage and he forbid me from joining the family vacation, which was fine since I was over family vacations and didn't want to miss my shift at the radio station anyway. Plus, this punishment gave me the opportunity to throw a huge house party.

It was a wild one that required twenty-one garbage bags to clean up after. In a hungover haze, I picked up every last can, bottle, and cigarette butt . . . except one stray bobbie pin that had found its way to the parlor floor and eventually my mother's gaze. I got nailed and another beating ensued, but this would be the last one. As punishment, my mother tried to discipline me like she had done so many times in the past: by making me lie on the bed and belting the shit out of me. But I had finally reached a breaking point.

She had the belt out and was trying to whip me until I cried, but I knew it and refused to make a sound. Eventually she slowed down from exhaustion, and what happened next I am not proud of at all.

———————

My mother was breathing hard and still holding the belt, but her shoulders were slumped from all the work. It must have gone on for a few minutes for her to look like that, and she tried to give me one more lash, but it barely even hurt anymore. The anger was building inside me the whole time, and when it was finally over, I stood up straight as an arrow and turned around.

Staring daggers and feeling taller than I ever had before, I sarcastically asked if she was finished, and then pushed my mother against the wall and very calmly but forcefully told her, "If you ever try to hit me again, I will kill you."

I saw the blood leave her face as she realized I might actually do it, and then she turned and left. It was not as good a feeling as I thought it would be, but I knew we had just turned a corner. I had stood up for myself—finally. But when George came home that night and finished the job, beating the absolute shit out of me so bad I could hardly walk for a few days after, it was the last straw.

At seventeen, I ran away from home, and arrived in Atlanta looking for a taste of the hippie life. I sold a newspaper called The Great Speckled Bird (which would eventually become Creative Loafing) and even lived with fifteen other people in a communal house, but it didn't suit me.

After a few months I was back in West Point and had asked Dale to marry me, but the reaction was not positive—from her family or mine. Dale's father had previously caught us having sex and forbid her from seeing me, and George still didn't want anything to do with me. When I came back from Atlanta, he was so disappointed he actually told me I was welcome to visit my mother any time . . . but to make sure he wasn't home when I did.

All this weighed heavily on me, pushing me nearer and nearer to a nervous breakdown, so after a whole bunch of soul-searching, I decided our parents were probably right. Dale and I shouldn't get married, and I should go on to college like my stepfather had always wanted.

Sheepishly, I explained my plan to my mother. After we talked, she agreed. But it came with a caveat. "You should go down and tell George," she said.

She was right, and I felt good about it. I wanted to open up my soul and tell George I was wrong. I wanted to apologize and be forgiven. I wanted to feel like I had a dad. But he was asleep, and when he woke up, I was just standing there, nervous and crying. Sputtering, I told him the whole thing: That I would not marry Dale and that I knew he was right. And that I'd go to school instead and would even go wherever he wanted me to go. But he just sat up on the edge of the bed, shook his head, and said "Son, I am not your fucking money man. I don't care what you do."

It was too much.

At that point my whole horrid life with him flashed before my eyes, and the anger rose so quickly, it was one of only three times in my life that I went into a blind rage of my own. After all we had been through—all the times he coldly ignored me and I naturally rebelled, pulling farther away as the wedge drove deeper between us—he had finally broken me.

I think that pissed me off more than anything. I had come to him hat in hand and had completely caved, begging him for forgiveness and acceptance. And he could only think of my life as an expense line?

I blacked out, and all I remember is coming down the stairs with a loaded .410 shotgun. I was gonna kill the son of a bitch, and I didn't care about the consequences. I was tired of this guy's bullshit and some-where, deep in the back of my mind, I thought back to Bass's white-knuckled fingers, wrapped around that pistol grip in the car. George deserved it. I knew how to do this.

But as I reached the bottom of the stairs my mother stopped me. Trembling and desperate, she begged me, pleaded with me, and turned me around. She all but shoved me back up the stairs to unload the gun. Then I flashed back to running away from Bass years earlier, holding David's hand while mother fumbled with the phone and a madman with a gun screamed outside the door. But this time I was the madman.

I cried again. And she did too. We sat on the stairs like that for a while, crying together.

I didn't do it, thank goodness. And George never knew what almost happened. I think I'd probably still be in prison today if he did. But from that moment forward I was on my own, with nowhere to go and not a damn clue of anything except what I didn't want to be. I was pissed off and heartbroken and rejected from the only family I had ever known. I had no support system or experience with how life should be lived.

And honestly, I was scared.

PART 2

All By Myself

Behold, I stand at the door and knock. If anyone hears my voice and opens the door, I will come in to him and eat with him, and he with me. The one who conquers, I will grant him to sit with me on my throne, as I also conquered and sat down with my Father on his throne. He who has an ear, let him hear what the Spirit says to the churches.

Revelation 3:20–22 (ESV)

5

A Rocky Beginning

Most people can't point to the exact moment their childhood ended, but deep down I knew mine just had. There was no going back to West Point, and to be honest, a big part of me was glad. But then again, I wasn't prepared for what was coming.

My early trials with neglect and abuse were already secretly screaming in my ears like a million-watt speaker, and eventually, they would all but cave my head in, creating some serious havoc that would take decades to unload. But for now I was in the bliss of ignorance.

Just to show George up, I enrolled myself in LaGrange College—which had the added benefit of being an easy twenty-minute drive back to West Point and Dale's bed—but it was a stupid move. I had no interest in class and couldn't concentrate enough to get much out of it. I used to joke that the only book I ever read all the way through was Charlotte's Web, and today they'd probably say I had attention deficit disorder.

Studying never interested me, but now that it was on my dime, I quickly realized a college education wasn't required for a career in radio. What the hell did algebra and Shakespeare have to do with rock 'n' roll? Right?

In fact, all the time college took up was holding me back, so I enrolled myself in the School of Hard Knocks. I got a job at the local station,

WTRP, but with all the people I was meeting at school, there were plenty of distractions—mostly girls.

I couldn't see it at the time, but hooking up really was the number one goal for me. It was developing into a sickness and was always at the top of my mind. If I was around a girl, my thoughts were between her legs. What kind of panties does she have on? I wonder if I could get in the sack with her? I'm ashamed of that now, but if I became really good at anything during college, it was sex. Alcohol and the radio just provided a jumping-off point.

Soon I moved out of the dorms to save money, and from then on college was over. I made it three-quarters of school and then gave up, preferring to spend my time smoking pot, drinking, chasing girls, and listening to Frank Zappa with my roommate instead. It was actually a pretty tough time emotionally, since I had essentially proved George right about my chances in school. But I also felt like I was on to something bigger.

At WTRP, I started realizing I could pick the hits before they got that way. I could predict which songs would do well on the charts, and which wouldn't. It wasn't just about what I liked—it was something in-stinctual I still have trouble describing, but I knew if I could sharpen that instinct, I would have a shot at a long-term radio career.

The way I gauged "good" and "bad" was pretty simple. New music would come in all the time and any of the DJs could listen to it, but we couldn't just play whatever we wanted. The rotations were chosen by the music director and 27 director, and they had a lot of complicated reasons for the songs they chose. But I would make my picks in secret and then notice a week or two later that 90 percent of my stuff wound up on the Billboard chart.

That was proof enough for me to start trusting my gut, and I began to really believe I had an ear. "We Gotta Get You a Woman" by Todd

Rundgren was one of my early picks, and after it went Top 20, I became obsessed with practicing my craft.

Soon, I got a real shot at putting it to use. The station at LaGrange was getting sold, so I took a job at WXLE in Phoenix City, Alabama, just across the border from my boyhood home in Columbus. I was still low on the totem pole, but things started growing to the point where I was telling the program director which records we really needed to have—and I was relentless in doing so. To his credit, he ended up adding a lot of them, and when they did well, I was rewarded. I got my first morning show and was also named the station's music director, which meant I had some official say in what got played, and that was all big for me.

Music was my safe place—which is to say I could allow myself to feel whatever the song was about. That was hard for me in the real world, but at the station, I could pick music that would connect with people . . . and the music helped me connect to my own feelings as well as other people.

After never really feeling good at anything, I finally knew what I was good at. And even though it was a fledgling station that didn't mean much in the industry, it was a real job, and I had a real title. And soon I started bringing it some real attention.

There are thousands of radio stations across the country, but the ones that hold the clout are called "reporting stations." Those stations physically "report" the songs they play every day to industry magazines like Billboard and, at the time, Cashbox. And that's how the charts we talk about are actually made. Plus, back then, there were also independent publications like the Gavin Report and Friday Morning Quarterback (published out of New Jersey by a guy named Kal Rudman). There was opportunity to make yourself into a "reporter" if you could convince one of these publications you had your eye on the ball.

That's what I wanted to do with WXLE—I wanted to make us legit. And after a few months I got a big ole set of balls and made it happen.

By reading things like Friday Morning Quarterback, I could see what the other radio stations were playing and knew we were doing the same thing. In fact, we were often early on a hit, because I had picked it out. That type of thing would be huge if we were reporters, so I wrote to Mr. Rudman and basically blistered the whole industry. I started listing off all the records I had been first on, including a song called "Help Me" by Joni Mitchell which I was the very first DJ to spin. I let loose with a torrent of trash talk to get his attention.

"I don't understand how the FUCK I am not a reporter!" I wrote. "You have your head so far up your ASS! This whole system is BULLSHIT and you know it!"

Needless to say, it was a little over the line of professional decency . . . but it also worked. Within a few days I got a response that basically said, "Who the fuck did I think I was?" But even so, Rudman made me a reporter to Friday Morning Quarterback two weeks after that, and I started getting the attention of record-label people. I even got my first industry award for being the first DJ on board with "Help Me," and it was a milestone that really opened doors for my career. But my winding path was getting darker.

Things were good at work and bad at home—something that was becoming a pattern for me. I was still on again, off again with Dale. It was never ending with us, and almost all of it was my fault.

In keeping with my controlling nature, I always selfishly prided myself on making a breakup so miserable that the girl would do it for me, but at one point she got me pretty good. Dale left, and for some reason, this time it devastated me to the point where I went off into the woods and actually cut my wrists with a sharp rock. Not enough to be dangerous, but clearly a desperate cry for help that I kept anyone from hearing, and I still have the scars today.

She didn't stay gone, though, and we eventually got back together. Dale moved to Columbus to live with her cousin—and so did I. It really helped me out since I was only making seventy-five dollars a week, and she was available for sex any time I was there—but then the inevitable happened. She got pregnant, and my first marriage was under way. You gotta love a shotgun wedding.

We bounced around between the houses of a few friends until we finally found an apartment for seventy-fie dollars a month—and I remember surviving on beans and cornbread for the longest time . . . although there was always money for booze.

We were so broke we couldn't even afford maternity clothes, so Dale would wear my blue jeans and just cinch them up until she got so big they fit her. But eventually, Dale's dad came around and accepted that we were married (or maybe, more to the point, that he was going to have a grandchild), so he sent us some money to help buy a house.

Things were looking up, but I just couldn't let myself have a peaceful, loving relationship, and all the while, the rhythm of drunken nights was picking up. I went from a gentle waltz with whiskey every now and then to a nightly Jack Daniels' break dance, and unfortunately, when it comes to drinking I've always had two left feet.

We got into the new house and I swear it was like the baby could tell—because the next thing you know the little guy arrived. And things became real toxic, real quick.

A lot of it had to do with my extremely controlling mental state, and I think because our relationship started with the death of Dale's mother, I had assumed that parental-figure role for her. I was dictating what she could wear and how much makeup she could put on, but that wasn't the worst part. Even though I fooled around on her constantly, I had this thing in my head that she was cheating. Every day on the way home from work, I would imagine walking in and catching her, and the effect in real life was me coming through the door angry . . . infuriated, really.

Raging to myself in the car, I would drink heavily as I drove—just like my old friend Bass Lewis—and all while this fantasy of me catching her in the act would consume my mind. Predictably, I never caught her doing anything. Most likely she never did. But in my messed-up mindset, that somehow pissed me off too. Like she had lied to me in my thoughts.

I was acting like she couldn't do anything right, and walking in the house mad set us up for failure. I think now I was punishing her for my own guilty conscious, because it really all came from me and what I was doing. It was totally unfair and wrong, but I wouldn't understand that until much later.

In the end, the baby was born and we named him Jason—and soon, Dale decided she couldn't take it anymore. She took him and left for good. And honestly, how could she have stayed? I gave her no other choice. But even though I had just lost the love of my life and my first-born son, her leaving didn't really bother me. I had seen plenty of divorces before—including my mother's—and knew there'd be another girl to marry. I felt like I owed Dale nothing, and didn't think of Jason at all. I can't imagine being that person now.

I never saw Dale again, and I didn't see Jason until he was 19 years old. But our reunion was pure poetic justice. He came back into my life like a chip off the old block—by having an affair with my wife (don't worry, that story is coming).

6

Who's Next?

By this time I was barely even out of my teens, but my life was already a full-on circus, or maybe more like the backstage dressing room at a Zeppelin concert. I had let myself become my father just like my mother warned against—a cheater and a drunk who divorced his wife and walked out on his son. Looking back today, I often wonder if Jason felt the same abandonment I felt when my father vanished. But back then, none of this sad, guilt-riddled insanity slowed down my appetite for sex and drinking. I wasn't in the habit of processing trauma and wasn't going to start now. And once I almost got shot for it.

Some of the promotions we did for WXLE were crazy. The station itself was in Phoenix City and one time we did a live broadcast from a bar in nearby Columbus. I was drinking (obviously), and when the show was over I started drinking more. Soon enough, I was slow dancing with some random girl, and I can't even remember who asked who, but I do know our hips were pretty cozy and my brain was on full hook-up alert.

We went around and around for a while, and at one point, I went into the bathroom to take a piss. But while I was zipping my fly up, the stall door opened, and before I could mumble something about waiting his damn turn, I wheeled around to find a guy with a pistol in my face.

He had a dark, angry face with bloodshot eyes and sweat dripping from his brow, a crusty old shirt, and the smell of desperation that only comes from reaching rock-fucking bottom. The dude towered over me like a bear and was at least twice as wide, or at least it seemed, and I watched him cock the gun and put it right up to my nose.

Being at least half-cocked myself, I was having none of this shit.

"You don't want to do that, because I know judo," I said, somehow keeping a straight face. "And I'm gonna kick your ass."

It came out so cold that Clint Eastwood would have been proud, but it was a total bluff. I weighed all of 145 pounds, and suddenly needed to use that toilet again.

I did know a little judo, but only because I took lessons at YMCA camp as a kid, and there was absolutely no way in hell I would have survived that fight. But somehow I talked this guy out of shooting me. It turns out he was the girl's ex-husband, and I just happened to be in the wrong place at the wrong damn time.

After some begging, I finally convinced the guy to put the gun down and offered to buy him a drink. He said he'd take one, but threatened to kill me and everyone in the bar if I told anyone about the gun—so obviously, I kept my mouth shut. I don't know if I've ever been quite as scared in my life, but we ended up sitting at the bar for twenty-five minutes before he left. And then I took the girl home and slept with her anyway. So, not too bad of a Friday night.

Coming out of that bar alive, I should have been a changed man. For a few weeks after that I would wake up in a cold sweat and swear that guy was in my house, and I knew for sure I had almost gotten myself killed by messing around with a woman I shouldn't have been messing around with. But I actually met my next wife, Shelly, in a similar situation. Lighting doesn't strike twice, right?

Looking back now, I have no idea why we even got married. And that was just another piece of proof that I hadn't developed a healthy sense of what relationships were all about. I sure didn't witness any of that from my parents and have now come to think that the relationship between the parents themselves is even more important than the relationship between parent and child. That's what I was mimicking with my own relationships, and like my stint with Shelly, my mother always had a transactional approach to love.

With Shelly, I guess it went back to this half-baked idea that if we got married, I could have sex any time I wanted. I always joked, "If I was gonna have sex with somebody, then I should do the Southern thing—the right thing—and marry them." Well, you quickly realize that "sex any time" is not the case after you get married, and then you've got to figure out how to get out of that marriage so you can move on to the next conquest.

Shelly and I met while I was doing another remote broadcast—this time at a Kmart in Phoenix City—and luckily, there were no guns involved. But it was still dangerous. She was working at the customer service desk, and after we got into conversation, we ended up hooking up that night. I wasn't divorced from Dale yet, so I couldn't take her home. We also couldn't go to her house because she was divorced with a kid and lived with her mom. Instead, we drove to the radio-station transmitter site where the engineer, Toby, had a bed set up.

No, he wasn't a sex fiend like me. Sometimes he just had to stay at the transmitter site for long periods of time if we had a power outage back at the station, so that was my secret spot.

Shelly and I continued to go out, and after I got divorced from Dale, I moved in with her and her little boy, Glen. She was a Mormon, which was new for me, and after we got married we bought ourselves a mobile home, figuring happily-ever-after was right around the corner.

Here's a tip: don't ever buy a mobile home. Maybe it goes without say-ing now, but back then they seemed like a reasonable and modern way to live. It's a bad idea because you can't ever pay it off—the terms they give people make sure of that. And you can't sell it, either, because who the hell wants to buy a used trailer? But it's an even worse idea to move the damn thing to the next town . . . and that's what we did.

7

On Air, and On Coke

Not too long after we got married, I found out WHHY in Montgomery (the same station I visited as a kid) was looking for a music director. And since I had built relationships with some of the local record-label people who would be working with this new music director, they actually recommended me. I was surprised, but put a promotional tape together to officially apply—and I was even more surprised when I got the job, even though I wasn't a great on-air DJ.

I had only just married Shelly, and now we were looking to drag a mobile home to another city. But worse than that, I felt like I was dragging myself through the relationship. All three of us (Shelly, myself and the trailer) moved to Montgomery, but our little trio didn't last long at all. More to the point, I didn't last long. What it came down to was, I just didn't love Shelly, and as a bonus, I got stuck with a kid at the same time. She was cute and it was an okay relationship, but I didn't want this for the rest of my life.

We broke up less than a year after moving to Montgomery, and I was now a twenty-year-old estranged father and a two-time divorcé. For the moment, I was content to stay single—in the eyes of the law anyway.

It was 1972, and I was the music director of a real-deal radio station—WHHY out of Montgomery, Alabama. It seemed like the big

time to me. I had listened to that station for three summers while working at YMCA camp, and was even inspired to create the name Lanny
West by one of its DJs. It was a cool full-circle moment, and even though
my personal life was a mess, I felt on top of the world.

I was still living in that God forsaken trailer, though—complete with
shag carpet, fake wooden beams, velvet paintings, and a bed I cus-
tomized for hookups. It had speakers in the head board and storage in
the footboard for vinyl albums. It was proof that I was a total sex pistol,
right?

It had to be true, though, because hooking up was really easy—and I
don't mean that as a boast. In my opinion, it was easy because the girls
wanted to hook up, especially with DJs. So I had girls call me at the station asking to come meet me all the time, and I'd end up taking them to
the trailer for a romp and never seeing them again. I think they enjoyed
the thrill of it all as much as I did.

My favorite hookup line was straight to the point, and nine times out of
ten, it was successful. I would wait for a quiet beat, lock eyes, and just
say, "What would you think about coming home with me and taking a
shower together?" And boom! I was in. None of those stupid "heaven
must be missing an angel" things. I just got right to it and asked for what
I wanted, and I think maybe they appreciated that more than any other
cheeseball line.

But even with all the sex and drinking, I was actually determined to
focus on work. My position at WHHY was once again music director—but with a much bigger platform than I had back at WXLE. I
worked for a guy named Larry who was the program director.

Midnight to 6 a.m. was my mind-numbing on-air shift, and beyond
that, my job was to field calls from record companies and listen to the
music they wanted played. Every Monday, I would gather all my re-

search and the music I had listened to, go over to Larry's house, and we would listen to it and talk over what we were adding to the station's playlist. Because I was the music director, I did all the research of calling record stores in the area, gathering sales information and pulling all the request documentation from other DJs. Then I would call the record label reps and tell them what we were adding for the week. It was an important job, and I was good at it right away. But that was kind of a problem.

Back then, we were hands down the biggest station in the area and a true Top 40 station, playing everything from Paul Davis and Helen Reddy to Charley Pride and Charlie Rich. We played whatever was hot on the chart —and in the '70s, it really was a true mixture. But Larry liked to flex his power and ran WHHY with an iron fist. So as I got more and more attention from the record reps, we were set on a collision course.

Once, he went on vacation and actually allowed me to do the music by myself, and naturally, I jumped at the chance. I added a song by Paul Davis called "I Go Crazy." While I was on the air doing my shift, I got a phone call. It was on the hot line, which was never a good thing, and to my complete lack of surprise, it was Larry.

"Lanny, what is that piece of SHIT I just heard on the radio?" he said. He must have been driving back from vacation and decided to pull over and cuss me out from a pay phone. A cold chill went down my spine. In my head I was going, "You asshole—you gave me the authority to add what I wanted." But at the time I just apologized. He couldn't remove it from rotation without explaining why to the label, though, so it stayed. And I got my revenge when "I Go Crazy" turned out to be a Top 10 Billboard hit.

Soon Larry couldn't work with me at all, so he pushed me over to the station's FM signal, which I think he considered a death sentence at the time. FM was the red-headed stepchild of radio back then and our station was automated, meaning it would just play music and commercials from a mechanical carousel—no DJ needed. But I turned it into a monster that kicked everyone's ass—Larry's included. It's a good thing, too, because it turns out he was trying to get me fired. I was only saved when the FM sales manager, Wiley, suggested he could make some money for the station by changing the FM side to a live format.

Unfortunately for Larry, it worked far better than anybody predicted, and unfortunately for me, it turned out be a double-edged sword. I was climbing the metaphorical charts of my career, but also ended up descending into some of my darkest days. And if you've made it this far into my story, you know that's saying something.

You see, Larry was the top dog at WHHY, and because of that, he had a lot of pull in the Montgomery community and with many of the record labels. But there was a disconnect—the record-label people would come to town looking to grease palms and do whatever it took to get their music added. But Larry wouldn't go out with them at night because he had a family.

But me? I was always up for a night out.

We'd do some drinking, do some carousing, talk some shop, and generally rock Montgomery like we owned the place. And then someone busted out the cocaine, and it stayed out for years and years.

———————

After I took WHHY's FM station live, I was out and about in Montgomery all the time, taking record label guys to restaurants and bars where they picked up the always-hefty tab. There was a Ramada Inn in town that had a club inside, and I brought that place so much business by recommending it to record people that I could basically do whatever I wanted.

It was the kind of club that had a pretty strict dress code, and this was disco dancing in its prime. Everybody went out in something flashy, but I could waltz in wearing jeans and a T-shirt just because of "who I was" in town. Everywhere I went I was getting free drinks, free haircuts, free meals. I was starting to become a bit of a local celebrity, and I was starting to believe my own hype.

At this point, you may ask why a mid-level radio guy in a mid-sized city would be of any interest to the big record labels at all. Well, back then we didn't have the Internet, and radio support made a big difference in those record companies' bottom line—a BIG difference. But it also went beyond that. Back then every station made its own programming decisions too (which isn't really the case anymore), so each one could theoretically be persuaded.

Here's the gist. Stations were split up according to market size—small, medium and large. A large-market station would be in a place like Atlanta or New York City, a medium-market station would be like WHHY in Montgomery, and a small market would be in a place like Eclectic, Alabama, which has a population of around 1,000.

What would happen is the large-market stations rarely (if ever) introduced new music. Instead, they watched trends in the other markets around the country and tried to pick out songs that already looked like winners. They had too big of a listening audience to take chances alienating the base with a dud.

My station, on the other hand, was in the business of breaking new music. WHHY was a medium-market station, and we were the number one station in the area. We had the majority of listeners in central Alabama tuning in, and we reported the songs we added to Billboard, Cashbox, Friday Morning Quarterback, the Gavin Report and more, so all the other markets were watching what we did. We also had a good track record of songs we picked becoming hits, so the major markets were influenced to follow our lead. It became really important for a record company to get their stuff on WHHY. Repeat this situation all over the country, and you have an idea of the radio industry at the time.

With us playing a brand new track from somebody like Mac McAnally, for example, a record-label guy could walk into any major-market station and go, "Look, here's what's happening in Montgomery. These are the local sales numbers and the requests they're getting. You need to add this for us." Then, if the major markets did add it, that took the song to another level commercially. The labels figured out they could spend some time and money greasing wheels at the smaller stations and potentially gross millions in sales on the back end.

So that's what made us important, and since I was one of the two people responsible for adding new songs, I was the wheel the labels were looking to grease. Did I believe these guys actually liked me? Some of them did, and we are still friends today. But most of them sucked up to me and brought me drugs and took me out to dinner because they wanted their record played on my station.

The problem was that it kind of went to my head, even though I knew deep down I was a pawn in this much bigger chess match. I felt like a star in Montgomery, and that's what I secretly always wanted, going back to my first taste of radio in high school. But the more connections I made, the more control I lost.

Our FM station was exploding in popularity, and with that, came a never-ending stream of record promoters. And this was the '70s, so cocaine was literally everywhere. It was a standard part of doing business, and my guys would sometimes show up with an ounce of blow or more to match whatever music they were pushing. And whatever they brought, we would do. I used to joke with people that I did more blow than they could bring in from Columbia.

In the early days, we'd do our cocaine over at my place. Or in one of the their hotel rooms. If we went out to a bar, they'd give me a little vial and we'd go toot it up in the bathroom. You had to be careful because you obviously didn't want to go to jail, but it was pretty much wide open in the nightlife crowd. I quickly realized it was good for getting sex, too, because girls loved it. And if you had it, you were a rock star.

Cocaine was the thing, the tool, and it led to a lot of dangerous stories, especially when coupled with alcohol. They say it makes a new person out of you, and that person might seem cool (even brilliant) at first. But really, he's just a fiend who wants more cocaine.

There are wild stories of pop superstar Elton John not sleeping for days at a time back in the '70s, because he couldn't go to bed knowing there was more coke in the house. He was hardly alone. All the stars were doing it. It was even supposedly non-addictive, but we all knew that wasn't true.

I wasn't on Elton's level (I didn't have his kind of access to the stuff), but I loved it from the start. It didn't jack me up like it did most people. There was no teeth grinding or wild eyes when I did cocaine. It actually made me a little more withdrawn and relaxed. But I will tell you this: doing cocaine and matching that with sex was something else. Something way more intense.

I started off slow, and at first, I'd just do cocaine whenever I could get it. There's this weird unspoken rule where everybody at the party knows it's coming out eventually, but you don't want to ask for it. Soon the coke became part of a pattern and it didn't take long before I was actively looking for it, doing it every day if I could. And then I started looking forward to when certain record people would come to town, because I knew they would have it. Or I would make sure I was sent to events in Atlanta or Los Angeles where I knew how to get some.

Even if my usual contacts weren't around, it was easy to get on the street. The stuff just blanketed my whole world like a snowstorm. I was having more fun, more success, and more sex than ever. So, on the one hand, things were looking up. But the coke also came with a price tag, and I don't mean the going rate of a hundred dollars a gram.

Within a year, my sinuses were wrecked. I consider the issues I have with them today as the thorn in my flesh that I'm punished with for abusing myself. It got to the point where I'd stay out partying all night, and then I'd have to drink Nyquil or smoke pot to bring myself down enough to get to sleep at four in the morning. Then I'd have to get up at eight or nine and be on the radio by ten. Trying to function that way all day meant I had to do more cocaine just to keep myself moving.

But one night it all came to a head.

8

Into The Shadows

Cocaine was everywhere in my world, and it wasn't just me. Being in radio in the '70s, doing a little coke was like going out for lunch—it was just part of your day. But that doesn't mean your body could keep up.

At one point my sinuses were so bad, I remember driving into the trailer park and throwing a vial of cocaine into the bushes. It had about three grams in it, which was worth $300, but I couldn't take it anymore. I was crying as I got into my trailer. How did I get like this? I couldn't breathe. I couldn't sleep. The mood swings were wild. I was standing on my head trying to get my nose to drain, but my sinuses were swollen so bad it was no use. All I could think about was being a failure, and once again proving my mother right. I really was turning out to be a loser just like my dad.

I swore off cocaine that night and really, honestly meant it. This was no way to live. But when I got up the next morning, it was like nothing happened. To the part of my brain that wanted more coke, the things I felt the night before didn't matter. It just wanted a fix—and I knew right where to get one. I stopped in the bushes and found that cocaine on my way to the station and started doing it all over again. The stuff was irresistible.

Eventually, though, even the coke wasn't enough, and soon I ventured into speed and quaaludes. Still, I didn't miss a beat at work, mostly because I really enjoyed what I was doing. But I will admit there were days when I could barely keep going. I was not doing myself any favors. Once, I even got myself into a quaalude-fueled orgy that had serious potential to ruin my career.

———————

It was late one night after an Atlanta Rhythm Section concert, and a friend, a record guy—both of whom shall remain nameless—and I went back to the record guy's apartment, but the guests of honor showed up a little later. Somebody, and it really wasn't me, called a group of hookers over, and we ended up having the kind of night only Keith Richards does twice.

Quaaludes were the thing at this party, but not really knowing what quaaludes do, I was also doing cocaine at the same time. And even though the result of that is not pretty, my friend and I ended up with three of these girls in the bedroom, and I'll just say it was a pretty debauched evening. That was the first time I was involved with another guy and multiple women, and from what I remember (which is not much), we all went wild. You might be wondering how I can say that, since I just admitted I can't remember. Much to our dismay, there turned out to be some physical evidence to go by, since the record guy took Polaroid pictures of the whole damn thing.

He said it was just a joke and kind of laughed it off, but my buddy and I freaked out. He was married and thought he'd lose his family. So, the record guy burned the pictures in front of us, and that was enough to put us at ease. But then a few months down the road, it started to seem like, well, maybe there were more pictures after all. He would say things like, "You might want to add this new record of ours. I wouldn't want to have to pull these pictures out." I was left to wonder if this was really blackmail or not!

It took a few decades before I finally learned the whole thing was just a big joke, and that there really were no more pictures, but that was a lesson that stuck with me. Shit happens when you party naked, especially with coworkers.

———————

All this coke I was getting was illegal on two fronts. Drugs were drugs, and even in the '70s we could get tossed in jail for possession. But me accepting them from the record guys was also a form of "payola." Technically, the radio guys were paying me with cocaine to play their songs on the radio. This "pay for play" practice was definitely illegal—but it happened all the time, and it wasn't just drugs.

They would do things like make your house payment, buy you a car, show up with TVs and video cameras, or book you a vacation. Anything you could think of. And it wouldn't be a thing like, "Hey, if you play this record, I'll fly you and your girlfriend to St. Thomas." They'd just do it, no questions asked.

In my case, they used the drugs for control, and a big reason they were willing to spend was how well the FM station was doing—now called Y102 and eating mercilessly into WHHY's market share.

Music was still the thing that made me feel like my best self, and I had put together a format for the station that was unlike anything else out there. It wasn't rock; it wasn't Top 40. I actually called it "Good Tracks Radio," and we stood out by playing way more than just singles.

I created this segment called Beechwood Park that came on every day just after lunch. It basically gave people an opportunity to record an entire album. I would have two copies of an LP by whatever artist I wanted, something like the Electric Light Orchestra or Steely Dan or Eric Clapton. We never played anything "wimpy." Even during the disco era when Saturday Night Fever came out, we refused to play one single disco song. We were the coolest thing Montgomery had ever seen.

The thing people loved was that once the show started, I would spin a whole album without stopping. I switched back and forth between records when one song was over, so there were no dead spots or commercials, and people could record the whole thing. Within six months, it was so popular I was able to add another live shift on top of my 10 a.m. to 2 p.m. show. And soon after that, I was able to take the station live 24/7. But that required a bit of trickery.

Y102 didn't have Arbitron ratings at the time—the complicated system that tracked listeners and told advertisers how many people were actually listening. We were still too fresh for Arbitron to have that data, but at the same time, we needed advertising money to keep it growing. So, I had to put something together to show those advertisers we had a solid audience, and what I came up with turned out to be pretty slick.

We did these promotions that got a ton of attention, and the first thing I created was called "The Secret Spot." My two-person sales team would tell me about a business they were trying to sell airtime to, and then we would do "The Secret Spot" right in front of that potential client's storefront.

We'd get on the air and announce this big, "secret" event for say, Friday afternoon at 5:30, and then give the location. All it really was, was a bunch of leftover albums, bumper stickers, T-shirts, and stuff like that we'd give away to the first few people in line. But without fail, people showed up in droves.

We never had less than 150, sometimes over 250 cars in line to get a prize. Once, we did a Secret Spot in Auburn, Alabama, that was so nuts the cops actually shut it down. The fact that so many people lined up outside a retailer's store, just because our station told them they could get a sticker, was worth more than a whole pile of Arbitron ratings. Those potential advertisers almost always signed up.

Another time, we booked an entire baseball stadium for the infamous "All-American Jell-O Jump," and it kind of became my calling card—even though I stole the idea from a radio station on the West Coast.

We had aligned ourselves with a local dairy, and the idea was to drum up some publicity for both of us. First, we made six hundred gallons of gelatin in fifty-gallon drums, and put them in cold storage for about a week. Then we built a sort-of swimming pool to hold it all, and the premise of the thing was that if you were selected, you got to get in the Jell-O and hunt for a prize.

The big prize we gave away? A stereo system. Not a car. Not a vacation. A stereo system. People will do anything for free shit.

We thought maybe a couple of hundred people would show up. It wasn't going to be huge. But we did pay to hold it at the AAA baseball stadium anyway, mostly because that made it sound like a big deal. And the city was on the same page—they let us do it because they didn't think anything crazy would happen, and we promised to donate some money to charity. Well, over twelve hundred people showed up for this damn thing, and the line of people hoping to jump in the Jell-O went around the stadium.

It was a problem and became news around the neighborhood. Soon, a bunch of kids were taunting people sitting in the stands. They started blaring music and throwing things up at our crowd, and then the people in the stands started throwing it back down on them too. The next thing you know we've got cops everywhere, and even the mayor showed up, forcing us to shut down. This thing caused so much trouble, it was actually great!

It made the newspapers as a riot, and we were forbidden from ever doing anything in the city again. They even proclaimed the stadium off-limits for anything like that in the future. But any publicity is good publicity, and I loved causing a stir. In fact, I came to learn that crazy, attention-grabbing promotions were sort of my specialty. But recently I've come to realize that "attention-seeking" might be a better term, and it showed up big time in both my personal life and career.

In fact, my time in radio taught me a lot of bad habits, and it really added fuel to the unstable parts of my behavior. But I was far from alone—the whole industry was caught in this cycle of debauchery.

PART 3

Friends In Low Places

And I said: "Woe is me! For I am lost; for I am a man of unclean lips, and I dwell in the midst of a people of unclean lips; for my eyes have seen the King, the LORD of hosts!

Isaiah 6:5 (ESV)

9

Just Part Of The Crowd

After a few years in the radio business, I had made a name for myself both on the air and behind the scenes, and also picked up some pretty questionable new habits. It was kind of like being in high school again and wanting badly to fit in with the cool kids—you just went with the flow and took your cues from the people who were higher up the social order than you. But I was nowhere near the worst of my kind.

There were these radio-and-record conventions that concentrated the bad behavior and unleashed it for days at a time. Every one that I attended was like an alternate universe—like once you walked through the doors of the hotel, the normal rules of society didn't apply. They were almost like fraternity initiations where anything goes, and in my search for some kind acceptance and self-worth, I lapped it up. I took the lessons learned at these things and ran with them, supercharging a tendency toward over-the-top self-indulgence I already nurtured.

There were lots of conventions, but the ones that stand out to me were the ones held by the trade magazines—ones like Friday Morning Quarterback or the Gavin Report. No matter who was running it, though, the basic premise was the same: get record companies together with radio programmers, so they could "learn how to better serve each other's needs," in person and all-at-once instead of little by little.

That was the public facade, anyway. In reality, these things were cash cows for the trade publications and another chance to grease radio's wheels for the record guys. But for radio programmers like me? They were another opportunity to live our wildest rock-star fantasies.

Here's what it was all about: The magazine would book a block of suites and rooms in a hotel somewhere, and then turn around and charge each record company a much higher rate to make one of those suites a base of operations. Just like any convention, there would be expert panels during the day and private parties in the suites at night, where record companies would schmooze radio people and demonstrate their latest "products" (in this case, new artists). But in the music industry of the 1970s, these conventions were basically a competition to see who could party the hardest.

Some of the suite parties would have DJs (I was even paid to DJ for a major label at one convention—talk about payola). Some would have fancy food and others would have hookers, but all of them had artists, drinks, and drugs. You'd drop into one room and there'd be a bunch of people huddled over a mirror on a coffee table, then go into another and there'd be five naked women just walking around with a line of men waiting to get into a mysterious back room.

There was so much cocaine at these things I don't know how anybody made it to the panels during the day, but for everybody with money involved, things worked out perfectly. The magazines made huge profits selling suites to the record companies. The record companies did actually get to introduce new artists and make important promotional contacts. The hotels were full of guests and made money catering the parties. And the guests? Well, guys like me had the time of our lives.

I was a young music director working for Larry when I started going to these things, and the one conference that stands out in my mind was my very first. The first time is always memorable, right? It was a Rudman convention in Atlanta at the old Stouffer's Inn. There was no easing into this crazy underworld—you just jumped in headfirst.

The Stouffer's Inn was cool because each suite was attached to a big swimming pool, and we put it to good use. Almost right after I arrived, I ran into two buddies who worked for record labels, and we had been doing cocaine and partying together in Montgomery for years. But this time was different. I went up to their suite with Larry and a few other radio people and a couple of label guys. Since it was the first night of the conference, they wanted to shock us.

The whole thing started with two older, well-known Atlanta industry guys—a station owner and a big-time artist manager (both will remain nameless). They decided to have themselves a little contest . . . to see which one could perform the best oral sex on a hooker who was hired for the weekend. That's right, folks, I had walked into a real-life pussy-eating contest!

I remember that Larry and a couple of others left before the contest began, leaving me and a handful of other younger, impressionable radio guys to watch and learn. And learn we did. A few quaaludes were offered to the girl and then she got comfortable, and the casual nature of it all still sticks in my mind.

I was completely flabbergasted. I had never seen or been a part of anything like this before. Even my own night with the hookers and the Polaroids was just a spur-of-the-moment thing, not an official work event. But regardless of my comfort level, this thing was happening. Each guy had up to five minutes to perform oral sex on the girl—in front of all of us, mind you—and afterwards she would pick who was best.

We just sat there in shock and watched this whole thing unfold, and although I don't remember who technically won in the end, it definitely skewed my moral compass. That moment helped set a tone about what was acceptable and expected of me as a man in this business, but remember, my moral compass was never really calibrated to begin with. I had just been pointed in the wrong direction, again.

That was the convention's opening event, but the weekend was far from over. The next night all the attendees went to see The Doobie Brothers at Georgia Tech. Then we all got together for another big after party, hosted by the band's label in the same suite where the contest was held the night before.

This time the place was packed, and the band was there to hang out. And so were many of the big-dog programmers from all around the country—really respected people in the industry. About three quarters of the way through this party, two guys suddenly emerged from the bedroom carrying the girl from the night before over their heads, butt-ass naked. They weaved her through the stunned crowd and dumped her in the swimming pool, and right away she set about trying to entice guys to come in after her.

At this point most of the "respectable" guests filtered out—and I should have taken my chance to do the same. But after what I'd seen the night before I figured, "Nah, this is fine," and soon the only people left were the real druggies and deviants (like me).

The scene was like something out of a porno flick, and there was cocaine literally everywhere. One guy was being held down by some label guys in a chair in the corner while the swimming-pool girl gave him a blow job. Another was so messed up he took a whole watermelon from the buffet, cut a hole in it, and started screwing it in front of everybody. I'm not kidding!

This party was totally out of control, and it isn't the way things are done anymore, but at the time it was pretty common. It may seem hard to believe now, but there was some logic to the madness.

I have to believe the convention culture didn't start off so insane. But if you were representing a record company, the whole point was to keep people in your suite as long as possible—and to keep them away from the other record companies' suites. You wanted to get them interested in your artists and help them decide to play that artist's music on the radio. To do that, you needed their attention. It was a no-holds-barred, shock-value kind of thing, and after that first experience, I started becoming even more detached from reality.

———————

Even though I was staying single, I had no trouble finding ways to use what I'd learned at that convention. I was still going out all the time—and that meant I was also hooking up left and right. Women would call the radio station to pick up the prizes they had won during call-in contests, and we'd often go back to my place for sex or even do it right there in storage room where the T-shirts were kept. I'm still not sure how I never got caught doing that. Another time, I started seeing a girl who was still in college, and after she got pregnant, we agreed she should get an abortion. At the time, it didn't even register in my mind as an issue.

There were tequila-drinking contests and countless nights where I'm not sure how I made it home from the bar, and I always wanted to see how far I could push things. It was like I wanted to impress people with my craziness—and especially the record company guys who were bringing in all the coke. I wanted them to tell stories about me, and I wanted them to want to hang out with me . . . all because I desperately wanted to be liked.

One time a record label friend of mine came to town with two other guys, and I set the "crazy" bar pretty high. We were out making our usual rounds, hitting the disco and a couple other favorite spots, but it was a quiet night and we quickly got bored.

"Well," I said, "There's a maximum security prison just outside of Montgomery, and I've heard that if you drive by real slow and turn your lights off, the two towers on the prison wall will spotlight you." It wasn't anything to screw around with—but dammit if we didn't screw around with it.

10

Pushing My Luck

So often while drinking and doing drugs, you do stupid things and regret it later. But this one could have gone way beyond regret. The plan was to drive by and test this urban legend out, but we wanted to make sure we got their attention. So before we got to the prison, just out of sight from the towers, we stopped the car and one of the guys got out.

He took off like a commando in the night, stealthily running into the woods and heading for the tree line where the forest ended and the prison grounds began. Meanwhile, we drove by the place like nothing was up, but then suddenly wheeled a U-turn and started back, cutting our lights and creeping along in full view of the prison wall. I could just imagine the guards in their towers squinting through the darkness, their hearts pounding as they tried to decide if this was a real escape attempt or not. And with me behind the wheel, it would be my ass on the line if they took the bait.

Sure enough, a blinding light soon tore through the side window, and just then our buddy came sprinting out of the woods and dove through an open window into the back seat. Other than the fact that he was in street clothes, it really must have looked like he had just escaped the prison. We took off like a bolt with screaming tires and a car load of idiots laughing our asses off. But it wasn't the smartest thing to do.

In very short order we had a state trooper on our bumper, and the laughing slowed down considerably as he pulled us over.

Unbelievably, we didn't go to jail that day. I was honest with the guy and told him what we had done, and it must have been obvious we were drinking. But when I gave him my license, it turned out he was a huge fan of Y102 and he knew who I was. We were let go with nothing more than a scolding.

I don't think anyone could get away with that today, and I can only shake my head at the risk we took. But at the time I was pretty proud of myself—I guess because I was confusing the thrill of an adrenaline rush with a real human connection. That lesson would take another three marriages to figure out.

———————

Every man is built from something. There's the raw material that he must be molded from, and the stuff I was made of seemed to require constant action. I could never stay still—or single—for very long. Even after a few close calls, like the one at the prison and that jilted ex-husband with the gun, I kept pushing harder. It was almost like there was something inside me that couldn't play it safe, and I accidentally learned that my father was the same way.

I came across some old papers, and to my amazement, I found that he wasn't a disgraced soldier after all. He was a real hero—once upon a time, at least. My dad had apparently seen some truly brutal combat in World War II and was awarded a Silver Star Medal for gallantry in action in Germany. The award said it was earned for his sheer bravery in commanding a tank and infantry formation that came under heavy fire. My dad had climbed up on a tank, completely exposed and with no cover, to direct his men to safety.

I was stunned, and I couldn't believe my mother had never told me this. I guess I figured she had her reasons, and maybe what he did later on was too much to forgive. But now, I wasn't sure what to think of him anymore. In any case, it made me wonder what had gone so wrong, and made me think maybe I wasn't so hopeless after all—maybe I could be brave too.

Around that time, my label buddy was back in town, and we got bored once again. As usual we had plenty of coke to go around, and we were headed out for dinner anyway, so I suggested a place I had been hanging around quite a bit. It was one of those spots where you'd walk in and everyone said hello.

I had been chatting with this waitress named Dockery for a few weeks, just flirting and making sure the record guys tipped her well—typical bullshit that made regular people like me feel like a big deal. But I was definitely angling for something more, and that night I hatched a plan that somehow worked. My friend and I were there alone, with Dockery and her best friend waiting on us, so I tried the ultimate big-shot move. When she came around I said, "Hey, we're gonna fly to New Orleans tonight, and we want you girls to go with us!"

It was total bullshit. We had no plans at all. But we said my friend had a private plane waiting at the airport, and we were just going to blow off some steam for the night. They actually believed us, which was awesome. But that meant we had to go through with it. Be careful with the bullshit you spew, kids! You just may have to produce.

It was getting late and now we had to find a plane—and a pilot—available for this trip. Luckily the set up wasn't totally fabricated. My buddy really did sometimes charter small planes out of Montgomery's airport, so he excused himself and made a few quick calls. And just like that, we had a plane to New Orleans. He put it on the label's tab and wrote it off like he was taking me to New Orleans to see one of the bands on the label . . . and eventually got in a whole shit load of trouble for the stunt. But for that night anyway, we felt like anything was possible.

Within a couple of hours the girls were off work and we were at the airport. And since we had enough blow to keep everyone higher than the jet stream, a few rounds of plane sex seemed like a real possibility. But we hadn't considered how scary a flight in a tiny prop plane in the middle of the night would be. And it didn't help that as we taxied out to the runway, the pilot suddenly stopped and got out. He went over to the right side engine and started tinkering around with something under the cowl. Then slammed it shut and had to fight with the latch to make it hold, and suddenly I realized what we were doing.

There were major warning lights flashing in my head, especially since a plane carrying the rock giants Lynyrd Skynyrd had just crashed and killed six people the year before—not more than a few hundred miles from this very airport. We were way too waxed to change our minds now, and luckily, the engine ran fine and the wings didn't fall off.

I breathed a sigh of relief as we landed in New Orleans and got into a car. We drove into the French Quarter and start partying, but the whole time I was on the clock. Remember, this thing was pulled out of my ass, and I had to be back in Montgomery for a radio shift at 10 a.m. So even though I still hadn't hooked up with Dockery, we hustled back to the airport just as the sun started coming up.

I was exhausted and drunk, and the only way I was going to make it through work was with some help. Luckily, my friend had that covered, too, and pulled out some Yellow Jacket pills used by truckers to stay awake on the road.

Gratefully, I went ahead and downed a big handful . . . right before he warned me to only take one and soon found out how useful that advice would have been. I must have seemed like a raving madman on the air and didn't sleep for another whole day.

Even though we had a great time and Dockery was impressed with my stunt, we didn't hook up that night in New Orleans. We never even got close, actually, but it started something between us. We began hanging out all the time after that, and built a whole relationship around non-stop drugs and sex. We ended up getting married a few months later (because I wanted to keep doing drugs and having sex, naturally) and I actually asked my cocaine dealer to be my best man.

I know. I can hardly believe that now, but it's true. I knew if he came, he would bring a whole pile of coke with him, and of course, he did . . . so we made use of it. To be honest, the sex, booze and drugs weren't even really fun anymore—they were like necessities. My whole lifestyle was like throwing a handful of sand into a canyon and expecting it to fill up. That canyon was actually the lack of real love in my life, and the sand was all the sex, alcohol and drugs I could get my hands on. I kept trying, but I never made a dent.

Dockery was my third wife and our marriage only lasted six months. There was no real depth to it after all, but it still made a lasting impression. One night, a couple of months after we got married, we had some friends over for a celebration, and after it seemed like everyone was gone, I sat down on the sofa to do some more cocaine and stare at the TV. But eventually, I realized I hadn't see Dockery in a while. That was weird, so I got up to look for her . . . and found her in bed with a girlfriend.

I honestly have no idea why it bothered me. Was I mad she was bisexual and didn't tell me? Or just pissed and jealous she didn't invite me to join? Either way I stormed out of the house in a rage, but not before using my van to push her friend's car out into the road. I had no problem hurting people who hurt me, but it could have been worse.

So naturally, I soon made it worse.

In a rare stroke of clarity, that night made me decide that doing so much cocaine was not actually helping me and Dockery. I think deep down I wanted to save the marriage and, once and for all, prove that I wasn't just a worse version of my dad. But I still had no idea what love was. Relationships were about sex and control to me, and this fight was about both. But regardless, enough was enough. So one night we made a pact to stop doing cocaine, and that was that.

I felt pretty good about it, too, but then the phone rang while we were in bed. And when Dockery came back, I could tell through the darkness something was up.

"Look, this friend of mine who I went to school with is coming through town," she said. "He's a guy I used to get my drugs from, but I'm not gonna do anything. He just needs a place to stay for tonight. Is it okay?"

I was skeptical but said yes—as long as no drugs were involved—and rolled over to go back to sleep. But almost as soon as this guy arrived, I could hear them doing cocaine in the living room. The sound was unmistakable, and my temper overtook me completely. For the second time in my life I went into a violent blackout. And this time, my mother was not around to stop me. I grabbed my pistol.

11

The Hits Keep Coming

The .38 revolver was cold and felt heavy for its size, but it fit easily in my hand. And once I picked it up, I had no idea what would happen next. I wasn't a gun nut or anything, and only had it because I was moonlighting as the manager of a local band. As a skinny white guy collecting door money from club owners in the middle of the night, you sometimes needed to make sure people saw it. But this wasn't a show-and-tell session, and I was beyond pissed. For a moment I tried to push the rage down, hoping to talk myself back into bed. But my mind was on fire, and as I saw it, she was blatantly disobeying me with some other guy in the very next room. The anger just kept rising.

My wife. In my house. What was next—were they gonna have sex? My fist tightened around the grip. A memory of Bass pounding on the door to my room flashed by, and then it was gone.

An instant later I was in the living room, standing there in my tighty whiteys and cocking the hammer on the pistol. Dockery and her friend both looked up, and I watched their faces turn as white as the coke on the table—the fear in her eyes telling me we'd never be together again. But I didn't care.

I stepped forward, shoved the gun right in the guy's face and gave him three choices. "I can blow your brains out right now," I said, not even recognizing my own voice. "You can leave and never contact us again. Or you can get the fuck out of here, and take this bitch with you."

He made his choice quickly and they both left, and as soon as they did, I slumped into a heap in the corner. I had no idea who that person was . . . and I wasn't thinking about the guy with Dockery. I meant me—the guy who just threatened to murder someone, basically for nothing.

In that moment of anger, I didn't even think twice about it and that terrified me the most. Once again, I had come close to crossing a line where there's no coming back from, and I couldn't trust myself to do better in the future. I wasn't even on drugs at the time, so what did that mean?

I spent that night asking questions like, What if you had pulled the trigger? Where would you be now? Is this really what happened between my mom and dad? The next day I sold the gun at a pawn shop, and all of it was enough to make me quit doing cocaine for a while. But unfortunately, not forever.

I may not have been good at marriage, but I learned it all from my mother. And even in middle age, she was setting the bar pretty high. She and George got divorced just before that awful episode with Dockery, but who knows why. I had left home years earlier and really didn't have anything to do with them. I never even came back to see her; I just sent Christmas cards. But still, the divorce rattled me.

Back when I was a kid, parents didn't think their relationships had much impact on their children. But here I was, a grown-ass man broken up because my mom's shitty third husband wanted her out.

She had moved from West Point to St. Simon's Island on the Georgia coast after the split, and that's when I finally reached out. We started chatting, and eventually, I went out to visit. At first it was good. We'd get along for a couple of days, but after that it was like pouring gas on a fire that never really went out.

Her health was an issue because she was taking medication but still drinking, and that was likely part of the divorce. But George is the one who got her hooked on those meds in the first place, prescribed to help her deal with chronic allergies.

The divorce was contested. George was taking mother to court and suing to stop paying alimony, because she was getting somewhere around $10,000 a month, including child support for their son, Mark, who was still a minor. I don't think I ever realized how much cash George was sitting on until then. I finally saw why my mother married him.

Well, you don't get rich by giving money away, and he put a whole case together to show the court she was an unfit mother so he could win custody of Mark. In my mind, it was simply a play to get the alimony and child support reduced or dismissed. Even though I had basically written her out of my life, it got to me.

I actually spent a good bit of time there going to court appearances—weeks really—and it was brutal. George had convinced my two stepbrothers, George and Bobby, plus my real brother, David, to testify against my mother. But as if that wasn't enough, they also brought Betty in to take the stand—sweet Betty the housekeeper who saved me when I got burned and had been part of the family for many years.

I found out from my mother that all three boys got new cars in the months leading up to the trial, but from the sound of what they had to say, the cars were unnecessary. They did everything they could to discredit her, saying she was a liar and abusive and that she drank way too much (which was not untrue). But they made her out to be this malicious villain, and thinking back now, that was probably her fault. I had gotten away from it, but they were all still surrounded by her issues, and it probably felt good to tell her off.

Even so, I couldn't stand seeing my family lie about my mother. Regardless of how I felt about her parenting, she had definitely been done an injustice, but she also wouldn't let me take the stand and testify on her behalf. She probably thought I would turn on her at the last second and join the other side, but I really just wanted to help. I'm not sure why. Maybe I just wanted to feel connected to her again.

Instead, I had to sit around and watch this tortuous process take place, and it was terrible. At the end of the trial, they didn't give George full custody over Mark, which he said he wanted. But they did reduce the alimony, so I figure his plan worked to perfection. I actually had to step in to help cover my mother's living expenses, and the whole thing had a disastrous effect on the relationship between me and my brothers. I disassociated myself from them and anyone who had anything to do with the divorce—more overreacting from a kid who can't process emotional wounds—and I never saw George again.

That was no huge loss, but it was twenty years later before I reconnected with David—and only then because mother had died.

I include this story because it speaks to the nature of love, as I now know it. Growing up, my mother didn't teach me how to love her or anyone else. But even so, the love was still inside my heart and soul, trying like hell to get out.

I think coming to my mother's side in her time of need was me trying to heal that old scar, and my life could have changed course right there. I could have got up on the stand and allowed myself to feel my pain and my love, in public and under oath. But it was another missed opportunity. I still didn't know how to love, and instead, I defaulted to rage by cutting my brothers out of my life for good. Somehow I knew what family was supposed to be, but I missed that experience in my own childhood, and now, I couldn't provide it for the women in my life, even when I tried. And eventually, I stopped trying entirely.

It wasn't long after I chased Dockery and her friend off with the gun that I was back on the market. Being desperate for affection will do that to you.

I met a woman named Diane through connections at WHHY, and we hit it off right away. Her father and uncles had built four very successful radio stations in the South—ones in Birmingham, Montgomery, Chattanooga, and Jacksonville—and we actually had a lot in common (for a change). She worked at the station in Montgomery, which was, at the time, the area's big 50,000-watt AM country music signal. And we both liked to party.

The sex was phenomenal, and she liked it almost as much as me . . . or maybe more. I mean, our first date was a no-holds-barred game of strip poker—and we both won. But since our stations were competing for ad money, it was kind of frowned upon for us to date, so we had to sneak around if we wanted to socialize in public.

Diane was as cute as a button, though, and forbidden fruit always tastes better. Plus, knowing we weren't supposed to be together made the sex even more exciting, at least in the beginning. Since I was still equating love with sex, you can see how I started thinking this relationship might stick. But it actually became the very reason we broke up.

Being in country music, Diane would travel to Nashville all the time for work. She would do interviews with artists and things like that, and she was always really passionate about that part of the work. It turns out she was passionate about hooking up with country singers too.

One day Diane admitted that during a recent trip to Nashville, she had given the singer Eddie Rabbit a blow job in her hotel room. I actually didn't even get mad this time and figured that was progress, right? I was still having sex with any woman who would have me—that was a given—so who was I to judge? I could let this one slide. I appreciated the honesty, and a few weeks later, I asked Diane to marry me.

Within a few months of meeting we got up in front of friends at the Episcopal church near my mother's place on St. Simons Island (even though I still wasn't the least bit religious) and started into my fourth marriage.

We got along okay. It wasn't as tumultuous as Dockery or as indifferent as Shelly, but it was the definition of insanity. I kept doing the same thing and expecting a different result. All of my relationships started out physical, and none of them involved getting to know the other person or becoming friends before we married. I didn't know or care what was in their minds; it was just what was between their legs. So when reality kicked in, I inevitably found out we weren't compatible.

I was also still having affairs any time I had the opportunity, and I got pretty good a juggling the lies. But this time my wife was cheating as well, and eventually, the balance started swinging toward those other relationships. Both of us were too interested in having sex with other people, so we agreed it wasn't working. The marriage only lasted about a year—again.

I wasn't even thirty years old yet and was already four-times divorced. But on the bright side, I had just experienced the most mature breakup of my life, if that means anything.

You know how sometimes it seems like nothing changes for a very long time, and then everything changes all at once? That's what it felt like after Diane.

I vowed to stop getting married, but that wasn't all. I was tired of the radio industry and looking for something different in my career. Over time, I had picked up on the way relationships and influence were the actual currency changing hands in the entertainment biz. Those crazy conventions were proof enough of that. So gradually, I started applying what I had learned. I met a ton of other radio programmers over the years, and when I decided to leave radio behind, I used those connections to make some seriously big money.

I was done with working directly for radio stations by about 1979. It was clear Larry was jealous of anybody else who had ambition, and I just knew he would stand in my way at every turn. As I looked around, I realized that most people in the business were constantly moving from one town to the next, climbing up the corporate ladder. But that life didn't really appeal to me. I had met a few "independent record promoters" over the years, and that was a lifestyle that looked good.

These were the guys who drove the fastest, most expensive cars and wore the flashiest clothes. If you were a young music director in a mid-level radio market like me, these were the guys who would stick a wad of twenties in your pocket for lunch when no one was looking. They would hear you were into making home movies and show up with a brand-new video camera and just hand it to you. They'd book vacations and even pay a utility bill.

Officially, it was all just out of the goodness of their hearts. But in reality, they were the shady characters who made sure pay-for-play was still happening.

Independent promotion wasn't really a traditional job—not like one you'd get anywhere else, anyway. They got paid for the relationships they built with people in the radio business—because those relationships gave them influence. And every time a station they were working added one of their records, they made big, easy money.

I had been one of those radio people for a time. Promoters had given me gifts to get a record on the air. And now? Now I was on the other side of it, ready to persuade my friends that "Such-and-such record is really good, you should add it!" (And "Oh by the way, I picked up those hi-fi speakers you had your eye on. Enjoy!")

I knew a lot of radio people in the Southeast by then, so I went to work for one of these promotion outfits, used my connections and made some of that big, easy money. But it just made somebody who was already stupid, even more stupid. And someone who was desperate for love even more paranoid of his self-worth.

By the time I was twenty-seven, I was making $125,000 (in late '70s money), had two cars (a Datsun 240Z sports car and a big conversion van), and thought I was a total hot shot. I had never seen so much money in my life. I mean, the most I ever made working in radio was about $350 a week, so I partied hard.

The cocaine use ticked up again, and my moral standards were way down. While I was in radio, I was careful not to do business with these indie promoters. I knew it was wrong to sell yourself out like that. But now that I was on the other side? It was game on! This was another piece of evidence that I didn't even love myself.

Looking back, I think I expected to feel bad about what I was doing, but I just never did. Probably because I was having too much fun. I was out drinking and picking up women every single night in Montgomery and all over the South—plus moonlighting as a party DJ I called "The Disco Wild Man," who was just as insane as the name sounds. I was also promoting local concerts on the side.

In fact, I had learned that putting a concert together was one of the most satisfying things I could do, professionally speaking, and I began doing it more and more. There are so many moving parts to a concert, and when it all comes together, you get a real feeling of accomplishment, and you get to hear some great live music.

Even while I was working in radio, I was putting small shows together. A coworker and I would book things like a high school auditorium for the jazz-fusion band Sea Level. I really looked up to the big promoter in the area back then—a guy out of Atlanta named Alex Cooley who did all the big shows with all the big names. As I moved on from my career in radio, I wanted to be Alex Cooley. But instead, I met Gary.

12

The Live Concert Game

Here I am, single again, still not quite thirty, and flush with cash like I had never seen before. My romantic life was in disarray, which was the only way I knew for it to be, and I was done with radio for good. But my old passion for music was just as strong. It was still the one thing I could count on. Even though I didn't know where my life was headed, I knew it had to involve music.

Luckily, I got put in touch with Alex Cooley's promotion company through some record label friends, and they helped make sure I stayed in the industry. Right off the bat, they hired me for this concert at a camping ground in central Alabama, and it was actually way cooler than it sounds.

The place was called Sandy Creek. It was really just some farmland off a single lane dirt road, sort of a Woodstock for the South with way less name recognition. But it often drew big crowds, and we were about to bring in ZZ Top and Alvin Lee. Needless to say, I was ecstatic about the gig. On top of that, I was in charge of everything from getting the stage built to renting porta potties.

But this first shot was not without its drama.

For starters, it rained and rained, and the dirt road got clogged up with cars stuck up to their fenders in mud. We couldn't get anyone in or out and actually had to arrange for a helicopter to bring ZZ Top to the stage.

They landed in a field full of cows which scattered like roaches at the very last second. It was pretty hilarious, and must have felt haphazard to the bands, but the show went off without a hitch.

I had done my job well and saved a bunch of money on the front end—and everyone likes a guy who comes in under budget. Stages are expensive, so I had the bright idea not to use one. Instead, we'd use flatbed trailers owned by some local semi-truck drivers, who I realized didn't haul on the weekends and would probably love some extra cash. It would be way cheaper to rent those than build a real stage, so we just drove the trucks out there, lashed the flatbeds together, laid down a bunch of plywood, and used some hay bales as stage barriers. It worked!

Despite the rain, the concert went great and made money. I got my fee and everybody was happy, so I started thinking I could be good at this job. I always knew how to anticipate needs—it was a survival skill to avoid beatings in my childhood—and I definitely had a promotional flair. So I guess word started getting around.

Looking back now, I must have been so easy to mark. I was totally defenseless and naive. All someone had to do was compliment me a few times and I would follow them anywhere—and Gary did just that. With what I know now, I would never have trusted his kindness, but I didn't see it at the time. And that's how he wanted it.

It was just another night at Cowboy for me, one of probably a hundred I spent at the club in Montgomery over the years, but this one was ultimately life-changing. I was sitting at the bar when a random guy sat down next to me, and it turned out we both had an interest in promoting concerts. What an amazing coincidence! Gary and I were instant friends and drank all night. We even exchanged numbers since he was new in town and could use a buddy in the business.

Over a couple of lunches we talked more, mostly about music and the local concert scene. Eventually Gary got around to mentioning something interesting. He actually had a big-money client looking to do big concerts and just needed someone like me to run things on the ground. Another amazing twist of fate!

This was like music to my ears, and before I knew it, we had drawn up plans for a company called Phantom Concerts to start doing local shows around Montgomery. Gary obviously knew what he was doing, because everything seemed on the up and up . . . I was a lucky guy!

After a few small shows, Gary had me convinced he was legit, so it was time for a bigger job—but first, I had to meet the boss. We went down to Sarasota, Florida, to meet Gary's money partner, and this guy had an amazing house on the beach. It was a mansion like nothing I had ever seen, really impressive. But apparently he was also an ex-heroin addict who was taking Dilaudid all the time—the stuff addicts get prescribed to ween them off the real stuff. For some reason, nothing weird registered in my mind, and maybe that's because there was plenty of cocaine around for me to partake in, so who was I to judge?

Even so, when we finally got around to business, it really did sound like one of those "too good to be true" situations. But I was new to the business and didn't have the experience to know what was normal and what wasn't. Apparently, they had a pile of money set aside and wanted to invest it in the biggest concert Montgomery had ever seen, and with stars in my eyes, I was like, "Hell, yeah!" I was so excited that I took the bait right away and said, "Yeah, I can help with that." And when we got back to Alabama, I used my contacts to get to work.

First, I contracted the Montgomery Motor Speedway, which was like a NASCAR short track, and went around finding motor homes to rent for the bands to use as dressing rooms and our office. We booked five or six bands in total with Molly Hatchet headlining, plus Leon Russel, Pure Prairie League, Mother's Finest—some really big names for the time. But we set the whole thing up in three days flat, doing coke the whole time, and we were flying by the seat of our pants. So there were some problems.

I was too stupid to realize I'd need to arrange for parking in the area. Or that we would need perimeter fencing because people will just walk in without paying. And those are just two examples.

The roads around the track were clogged with cars parking anywhere they could, even though I could easily have cut a deal with some of the surrounding farmers if I had thought to. But I had absolutely no idea how big this was going to be. Traffic got so bad coming in that the State Troopers eventually shut down the road coming in off the Interstate. And people did get in without paying, so I had to send security to various parts of the property.

While it was happening, the whole thing felt like a shit show, and I was convinced it would crash and burn. But overall, the show went well. The bands played and the crowd loved it. What else is there? Well, it turns out there's a little more.

We got to the end of the night and it was time to pay everybody out, and thankfully, spirits were high. We had weathered the storm and there was money to go around, so everyone was happy. But the stagehands were the last on the list to get paid, and their wages were complicated by the friends they brought on as my added "security."

I was busy figuring all of that out, then, all of a sudden and without any warning, a helicopter swoops in overhead and lands in a field nearby. And it wasn't a typical, slow-and-steady descent. This guy dropped out of the sky like a rock.

But that wasn't the strangest part. I looked over and what do I see, but my "friend" Gary sprinting to the helicopter like an overweight James Bond.

What the fuck? I thought.

———————

This was all wrong. I was in charge of this whole show and did not have a helicopter scheduled for any reason. The bands were already paid and gone. What the hell is this? But before I could make sense of the scene, it was too late. The chopper had barely touched down when Gary jumped in, heaving in a briefcase before him, and they took off like the Viet Cong was hot on their tail. Everyone was confused and looking around . . . then looking at me. And it hit me: that sleazeball had just taken the rest of our money.

I went to check the little office we had set up, and sure enough, Gary took everything that wasn't nailed down, or at least, everything that was left after the bands got paid. I had no money to pay the stagehands, and needless to say, they would not be happy. The realization hit me like a ton of bricks: Gary and his boss were not really interested in the concert. They were actually running a money laundering scheme, and I had just been conned. I was screwed in a big way.

The stagehands figured out what was going on at the same time I did, and soon, had me surrounded behind the stage. One of them even pulled a gun, and these were tough guys who had just worked their asses off expecting a payday, so I had no trouble believing it when they explained the new deal: I would pay them, or they would shoot me.

I did my best to explain what happened and that I was getting screwed too. I pleaded with them to let me find Gary. But that was easier said than done.

When I finally tracked him down, it turned out he had gone back to Montgomery and was staying at a hotel . . . the Ramada Inn of all places. It took some desperate groveling, but eventually, I found out what room he was in and went up there with fingers crossed. But naturally, he wouldn't let me in and had no intention of giving back the money.

It wasn't his to begin with, he said. It was the Florida guy's, and his neck was on the line. The only course of action I had was to call the sheriff's office and get them over there, assuming Gary would have drugs on him and get busted. But that only partially worked.

The cops couldn't just raid his room without cause, but they did convince him to give up enough money for me to pay the stagehands. At least I wouldn't get shot, I figured, but it hurt to know I was the dumbass who had just helped a probable drug dealer clean up his money (and add a little extra on top).

Gary flew back to Florida the next morning, and I was left to deal with the aftermath. I was completely distraught. I still owed money for all the staging, all the motor homes and trailers, equipment we rented, and what seemed like a thousand more little things. It was a lot of money.

All I could do was go home and sober up. Three days later, when I came out of the drugged-up stupor I'd been living in and got my shit together, I started working to pay it all back. It took me three years and I used up all the money I could make doing radio promotion, but it taught me some valuable lessons. First, that I had to quit mixing drugs and business. And second, not to be so desperate to be a big shot. Sometimes when you don't love yourself, all you want to do is impress people. And then you can't judge what's real and what's not—and that's how you get hurt.

I only saw Gary one time after that—in court when I tried to sue him for ripping me off. But I got nothing out of that either. His Florida boss had gotten him a good lawyer, so the only question he had to ask me on the stand was, "Were you and Gary business partners?" Of course I said yes since it was true, and in my head I figured that meant we should split the money 50/50. But in the state of Alabama, you can take the proceeds of a business without any notification to your partners, so he was free and clear.

PART 4

Saturday Night Fever

There is a way that seems right to a man, but its end is the way to death.
Proverbs 14:12 (ESV)

13

A Whole New World

I had gotten swindled bad by Gary and learned some pretty powerful lessons about who not to trust. But I still held out hope that I could build myself a better life, and I hoped I could meet someone to do that building with.

Even though I needed money and I had already been divorced four times, I was out in Montgomery every night looking to play the field. Cowboy was still my favorite spot, even though I met Gary there. But it was also where I could usually find a cute little waitress named Kathy.

It was a country-music club, so all the servers at Cowboy dressed in Western wear . . . and Kathy looked especially good in a hat and tight jeans. So I was always in there, buying champagne and leaving tips that were way too big considering my money situation. But in fact, being in Cowboy and hitting on Kathy all time actually helped me with that last part.

I needed a more stable job to go on top of the hit-and-miss radio promotion and found one spinning records at O'Charley's—the oldies bar downstairs from Cowboy in the Holiday Inn. It helped me seal the deal with Kathy and she would eventually marry me, becoming my fifth wife and my longest-lasting relationship to date. We even started a family together, but not before I met a businessman named Richard, who in some ways would play a bigger role in my life. He managed the Holiday Inn and also owned the Ramada, where I hung out a lot at Adam's

Disco. But he turned out to be more than just a boss. He was almost a father figure.

Richard saw something in me. He owned hotels in the Montgomery area and was also a regional manager for this Houston-based company called McFaddin Ventures, which owned or managed nearly 150 bars, restaurants, and hotels around the country. The Holiday Inn in Montgomery was just one of those and it was Richard who hired me to work at O'Charley's. Even though we were very different people, we hit it off right away.

Over the years, I had brought a lot of music industry types to stay at his hotels, so he was familiar with my reputation in the entertainment world. From my time in Montgomery radio, he knew I had a good sense of music. And after the concerts and all the crazy stuff we did at Y102, he also knew I had a lot of promotion experience, so he gave me a shot at something new. I was brought in to help program the club's music and give his team marketing ideas to freshen things up and get more publicity. When that went well, he led me into a whole new world.

Richard's office was actually in Atlanta, not Montgomery, and he asked me to come up there for a meeting. He needed to "show me something," he said cryptically. After getting burned by Gary and whoever that Florida gangster was, I was a little more skeptical this time, so I didn't get too excited. But that would change. This man was a straight shooter, and he told me what he wanted right away. McFaddin Ventures was planning to launch a new nightclub concept, Richard explained, and he thought I might be interested in helping.

We spent the day driving around Atlanta visiting different clubs that all had a theme of some kind—a disco popular with the gay community called Limelight; an oldies club called Studebaker's; a classic 1950's club called Johnny's Hideaway. And then he came out and said it: "I want you to put something together that will kick all of their asses."

By the time we got to dinner that night I had fallen in love with Richard . . . professionally, of course. He didn't jack me around and he seemed to respect me. He told me what he wanted, told me what he would pay, and most of all, he seemed to believe in me. After so many years of not having an older guy to look up to, I started thinking that maybe he was one I could count on. It was a good feeling. At the end of that first night we signed a deal on a napkin—the first of three deals we would eventually make like that. I wish I had kept those napkins.

The club Richard described to me was called Confetti, and it was supposed to be like New Year's Eve every single night. The positioning line was, "The Never-Ending, Ever-Changing Party." I would put together the music format and handle all the advertising and promotional marketing. All the staff would be in costume and this thing was going to open in cities all over the U.S. It would prove to be absolutely insane.

In the fall of 1980, Kathy and I got married and moved to Atlanta, but right away, I was shipped off to McFaddin's corporate headquarters in Houston to learn about the plan and get my piece of it moving. I spent hours and hours and hours calculating the beats per minute (BPMs) of every song in the format and cataloging the entire music library. Plus, I started testing the music out in one of the clubs that McFaddin owned there in Houston. This was the real deal, not the fly-by-night operations I was used to.

It felt good to be believed in, and for the first time in a long time, it made me want to do better. Once I started working in the club business, I got to use all of the talents I had. Understanding radio, advertising, promotions and knowing how to do live music events and how to energize a crowd—all of that stuff came into play. I poured my heart and soul into the work.

But as usual, I took it too far. I became addicted to the job just like I got addicted to cocaine. I was working way too much and never seeing

Kathy, drinking all the time and hardly sleeping. I guess in retrospect, I was almost perfectly suited for the nightclub business.

———————

Confetti opened its doors in March of 1981, and we immediately took over Atlanta's club scene. Inside the club, it was like time didn't exist. It really was New Year's Eve every night.

All the staff had to dress up in costume, from sexy tuxedo leotards to sexy nurses. It was always something sexy, and the dancing was just incredible. Disco was still really popular, so there were a lot of clubs with a great dancing scene, but Confetti was different. We figured out how to pace the night so people would stay and party for hours and not get bored or tired, and as a result, we started printing money.

I created a music format that was a hybrid of all the clubs in Atlanta at the time, and it basically created dancing all on its own. People just couldn't resist. It was everything from oldies from the '50s and '60s to the current disco hits, from hard funk like Rick James to new wave with Soft Cell's "Tainted Love." Just like any other club at the time, it got the dance floor going for sure. But I figured out a flaw in what everyone else was doing.

Their goal was to keep people on the floor indefinitely, dancing all the time. After all, they were out at a "dance club." But I knew we were actually in the liquor business, not the dancing business, and how do you make money at the bar if everybody's on the floor?

I realized that instead of constant dancing, what you want to do is intentionally clear the dance floor every now and then. You have to change the mood, change the tempo. You have to change the vibe and give people a cue that they should go get another drink so that's what I did.

My format did not have the same beat the whole night. I would take a hot disco song like Patrick Hernandez's "Born to Be Alive," which is about 130 beats per minute, and then I would switch it up with a classic slow song like Lenny Welch's "Since I Fell for You" or Mel Carter's "Hold Me, Thrill Me, Kiss Me."

Nobody else was playing slow songs—at all—but they didn't realize what dancing is all about. People don't go dancing just for the sake of dancing. They want to get together and simulate sex on the dance floor. And it's hard to grind if the music is all up-tempo.

I'd be in the DJ booth and once the slow song kicked in, I'd look around and people were either dry humping on the dance floor or going to get a drink. The money just rolled in. The guests loved it, and to make things even more interesting, we were always doing crazy skits that you might describe now as a flash mob.

We'd hire a high school marching band to come march and play through the club. Or a pair of actors who looked like the Blues Brothers to ride motorcycles in through the front door, through the club, and out onto the dance floor. You never knew what to expect and it gave us a reputation—and in the club business, that's better than gold.

We're talking about a converted Mexican restaurant with a dance floor wedged into what used to be an atrium, and we were doing $450,000 to $500,000 of business every month. Half a million dollars of Jello shots and vodka martinis! Sex really does sell.

In fact, we were always leveraging sex, and we'd do almost anything to get men and women together. We even turned Monday nights into one of our biggest money makers, and it was all because of sex.

Traditionally, Monday is a very slow day in the club business. Plus, Monday Night Football was (and still is) a big deal, so people would stay home. But we figured out a way to get guys to come in and spend money watching the game at the club instead. You'll never guess how, though, so I'll just tell you: it was male strippers and a ladies-only happy hour.

———————————

What we did was bring in a male strip group, kind of like Chippendales but from a local club called the Lemon Peel. These guys would come in pretty early and perform, and because of that, the club would be packed with women. We'd do dollar shooters of Deep Throats, Cum Shots, Blue Balls, all these crazy sex names. It was a full-on, highly produced strip show for women. But it ended at 9 p.m., right when the football game started.

During that whole time we would do a barbecue on the deck for the guys, but they weren't allowed inside the club while the show was going on. Then at nine when the strip show ended and the football game came on, we would open the doors and let the guys in, which was now full of horny women with a sizable buzz on.

It was like sex psychology with an extra boost. Since we were telling the guys they couldn't come in, and combining that with the fact the club was full of girls, they suddenly wanted to be there. Monday nights became one of our biggest weekdays, even though nothing had really changed but people's perception. It's crazy how that works.

Confetti was definitely fun and exciting, and I was glad to be out of Montgomery, but it was also hard to keep up with. We were open from 11 a.m. until 4 a.m. every day of the week, and I was usually there for about 12 hours on six of those days. And it was a club, so there was obviously drinking going on everywhere. But the temptations of drugs and sex were constant too.

That's kind of a given when your goal is to let customers simulate sex on the dance floor, but it applied to the staff as well.

Near the entrance, there was a secret little bathroom that only the staff were allowed to use, and our head door person had the key. But the regulars knew that if you tipped this guy enough, he'd open it up and let you in there to have sex or do some cocaine, whatever you wanted. The high-roller guests especially took advantage of this, but so did I.

Once in a while a friend would show up and ask if I wanted to do some blow, so I'd find someone to spin records for a while and we'd head into that bathroom. And there were at least two times I remember getting a blow job in the DJ booth while spinning records. My life was like the backstage of a Fleetwood Mac show, even at work.

I wasn't supposed to be drinking on the job—obviously. But nobody could really see into the DJ booth and it was right next to a bar, tucked back in the corner of the club near the dance floor. So I drank pretty much constantly. I'm sure Richard knew, because I'd be downing Jack and ginger and spinning records. I think he respected me too much to call me out. There were definitely mornings when I would wake up in my car after a long shift, and that was never a good feeling. I'd have to drive home and lie to Kathy, telling her it took a few extra hours to count all the money—but it really did take a while. We would close at 4 a.m. and sometimes not get out of there until seven.

For a guy like me, with my addictive personality and dysfunctional view on love, Confetti was a dangerous place. Every night offered the opportunity to drink until I couldn't take any more, and I took full advantage of that. On the plus side, at least my cocaine use had finally slowed down. After swearing it off a million times, I wasn't buying it any more—just doing it every once in a while if a friend had some. That doesn't sound like much, I know, but it was a step in the right direction.

But what never slowed down at all was my cheating.

Once the Atlanta Confetti location opened up and did so well, Richard's company decided to open locations all over the country. I was made brand manager for the whole Confetti concept, and McFadden Ventures moved me to Houston near corporate headquarters, with Kathy and the kids in tow. Justin had been born in 1982 and Jessica was on the way. But I was never home.

Over the next two years, I was on the road constantly, traveling between cities as we opened up twenty-eight more Confetti locations, and I made sure I had opportunities to hook up in each town. My sex drive came first, and I completely ignored the family that Kathy and I were building, even though it could have been my saving grace.

We were still in Atlanta when Kathy first got pregnant. We hadn't really been together that long, but she wanted kids and I figured, "What the hell?" The apple doesn't fall far from the tree, I guess. I was checked out from the beginning, just like my parents. Justin was born when I was thirty years old, then came Jessica in Houston. A few years later when we were back in Atlanta, Christopher arrived. Plus, I had Jason from my relationship with Dale, but I hadn't seen him since I was nineteen years old.

I had come a long way in my professional life, but judging from how I handled parenthood, I was still really damaged on the inside. I could have used my experience as the child of loveless, borderline negligent parents and made sure my own kids didn't go through the same struggle. I could have given them the father I always wanted. But I didn't. I just kept focusing on myself—on my own wants and desires—and I let my own family be secondary.

It's funny, because I think of myself now as a person who loves family. And back then I think I did too. But I found every reason possible to not be at home. Maybe there's some guilt tied up in there, or maybe deep down, I didn't think I'd be any good as a father. What little thought I did give parenthood was basically delusional, since I thought I was a better dad than the parents I had. But in hindsight, I wasn't better at all.

I would venture to say that when anybody grows up in a toxic environment, we all say things like "I'll never be like that, I'll never do that," but truthfully the bad behavior is all we know. If you don't have any guidance or teaching examples, you can say you want to do things differently all day long, but it's hard to hit a target you can't see.

I wasn't true to Kathy at all, and I showed no respect for her as a wife. When I was home and around her things seemed okay, from my perspective anyhow. But that was only about 10 percent of the time, and I would still take any and every opportunity to get laid.

14

Easy As Pie

It was 11 p.m. and the damn phone in my hotel room was ringing again. I was busy and in no mood to pick it up, but I had already let it go once. Something must be up. It had been two years of dingy hotel rooms and grinding through the opening of twenty-eight new Confetti locations in cities across America, and I was now officially fed up with life on the road. But one of the few places I enjoyed was Kansas City.

I was there a lot, but not because Kansas City was exciting or because that location needed help. I enjoyed the radio rep I hooked up with when I was there, so I asked her to excuse me and picked up the phone. It was Richard.

He knew how tired I was of traveling, and we had already talked about where he thought Confetti was heading. It became so popular, so fast that the ownership group was rushing new locations out, and it seemed to us like they were overextending. They didn't have time to train the staff and management properly so things were getting sloppy. Richard was ready to get out and wanted my help with something new.

"I want you to get on a plane tomorrow morning and fly to Atlanta," he said, adding in a flair of mystery. "I've got something to show you."

I was trashed, of course, but said, "Hell, yeah, I'll be there!" In the morning, I stumbled and staggered my way on to a plane at about 6 a.m.

Richard picked me up when I landed, and later that night he took me out, just like he did a few years before.

We ended up on Roswell Road just north of Atlanta proper, parked outside this place called Good Old Days. They did chicken wings and beer and it was just a place for college kids to hang out, but it was always slammed. We were sitting there doing exactly what everybody else was, having wings and a pitcher of beer (or two), but then Richard looked at me with this weird glimmer in his eye, and I couldn't resist.

"What?" I said, wiping buffalo sauce off my chin with the back of my hand.

He goes, "Lanny, I want you to look across the street."

So I did. There was an old boarded-up steakhouse with a giant cow on top of it. I was still lost.

He said, "I just leased that building, and I want you to help me put a club together that will put Good Old Days out of business."

Ohhhhhh. He had sold his stock in McFaddin Ventures and Confetti, and we were going to develop a new club called American Pie. It was basically Hooters with dancing, and it became one of the most successful concepts in Atlanta club history.

———————

With the way Richard brought me in and the relationship we had built, I thought he was giving me a free hand with American Pie. But as we got the place staffed up and ready to go, it became clear that wasn't the case. He also had two other guys in management roles who were involved in a few of his other hotels and clubs, and we were not exactly the three amigos. To put it mildly, they were assholes. These guys just didn't get the club business, but they had more experience than me, so when they wanted to do things "by the book," that's what happened.

Our grand opening was a big success. The place was packed and people were having a great time, but then it completely died. For the next three weeks, maybe a month, nothing happened. If we had ten people in the place at a time we were busy. Richard was freaking out and his guys were scratching their heads trying to figure out what was going on, but it was pretty obvious to me.

We had advertised the grand opening, so people were excited to come try this new place out. But we didn't give them any reason to come back. There are plenty of other places to dance and the chicken wings weren't anything special. So eventually, Richard had enough and sent the other guys packing and came to me with the message I was waiting to hear from the start.

"Lanny, it's yours now," he said. And I hit the ground running.

We started putting promotions together just like at Confetti, drumming up some curiosity. Our target customer was basically middle-aged pro-fessional dudes who owned Harley Davidsons, so we gave those guys a reason to come in.

We did Jimmy Buffett-themed nights and had parties on the deck. I had a DJ booth built in a perch overlooking the deck so I could spin records while the party went on. And crucially, we decided to zero in on another day just like we did at Confetti. This time it was Sunday, but it wasn't an attempt to get the after-church crowd. At the time, TGI Friday's down the street was where everyone went on Sunday. So we hatched out a plan to kill TGI Friday's.

You see, Atlanta had a big strip-club scene at the time. It got to the point where it almost wasn't taboo to hang out in one. But there was a simple reason for it all: in Atlanta, the girls could dance totally nude.

In most places, strippers have to wear a teddy or nipple pasties, something like that for "modesty." But in Atlanta, there was a law saying the dancers just had to wear "some form of clothing." They didn't say what kind. So the obvious choice was shoes, and this led to a whole region of guys who enjoy going to "shoe shows."

The clubs were hugely popular and seemed to pop up everywhere you looked, but fully nude or not, Atlanta's strip club scene did have one drawback: they all had to close on Sundays. We just figured out a way to take advantage of that.

It was simple, really. We knew nobody could go to strip clubs on Sundays. And we also knew that strippers would be out enjoying their day off and looking for a place to party. So we created what amounts to a rewards card—kind of like the ones you get at grocery stores now— and we went around to clubs handing them out to strippers. It let the cardholder and a female guest get into American Pie free on Sundays without paying the cover charge. It also got them two free drinks.

So on Sundays, American Pie was packed with off-duty strippers. And because of that, it was also packed with guys.

When we were getting all this set up, I remember Richard would call me every day and ask if we had a line of people waiting to get in yet. It was a joke at first, but all of a sudden the things we were doing started working.

I remember feeling like the first time we did $2,000 in one-day sales was monumental, and after that, the doors just blew open. On any given day of the week we would do $10,000 or $15,000 dollars, but Sundays were out of control. We would regularly gross anywhere from $55,000 to $60,000 on that one day alone—insane! And not only that, we had famous clientele as regulars.

Guys from the Atlanta Falcons football team. Baseball players for the Atlanta Braves were there a lot. Legend has it that Hall of Fame pitcher Tom Glavin actually met his wife at American Pie . . . but I'm not sure what day it was.

Richard kept letting me do my thing and eventually ended up promoting me to vice president, and I was feeling pretty big. It took me to a level of "Hollywood" that I always hoped I would get to, even more than the radio stuff or working with actual stars like ZZ Top. I lapped it up.

I would come in and start spinning records at 5 p.m. and I would keep going until 4 a.m., drinking way too much and working myself up into this performer's headspace. I had mostly gotten over my cocaine addiction, but I was still cheating on Kathy. Getting people dancing, making big piles of money (even if it was for someone else)—all of that was intoxicating in different ways. And with my addictive personality, it was easy to get lost in it.

But the reality check came soon enough.

15

A Glimpse Ahead

Throughout this book I've been caught in a struggle, a struggle against myself that I did not understand, and it clearly made me do some pretty crazy things. Writing it down and thinking through it now, a lot of it was dark and disturbing. But my life changed forever in 1987. I just didn't know it at the time.

The whole time I worked for Richard, whether it was at Confetti or American Pie, he also owned and operated a handful of hotels around the Southeast. And since some of them had clubs attached, he would often ask me to help promote them and check up on the operation.

I'd have to go to these places and help them get a new promotion set up, and it was just another part of the travel that was always keeping me away from Kathy and the kids. But I liked the feeling of power and superiority it gave me to fly in and boss people around, and sometimes I would even take it upon myself to go get involved.

One of those hotels, a Ramada Inn, was in Mobile, Alabama, and it had a deal going on with a local radio station. They were spending about $2,500 a month on radio advertising, which was a lot of money for Mobile. But part of the deal was that on Friday nights a DJ would set up in the club and broadcast live for a show they called Club 97.

It was supposed to get more people in the club, and it was working just fine, but I didn't like the DJ. He was kind of a cocky guy, not too different from myself, and I didn't like the music they were playing either. I wanted to make some changes in the format. After all, I had spent a long time in radio and thought of myself as successful in the club business, so I asked to meet with the station's program director and share some ideas.

I got to the station and was led into a conference room with the station's owner, the general sales manager, the national sales manager, the general manager, my own sales rep, and the music director, but the program director was nowhere to be found. I was, of course, a bit offended as we sat there waiting for about twenty minutes until, finally, this petite woman with dark hair and an air of steely confidence walked in and sat down right across from me.

I vividly remember feeling smug and ready to lay down the law on these people, and she had put herself right in my crosshairs. But she looked me straight in the eye and just said, "Hello, I'm Leslie. It's nice to meet you."

I don't know why, but I was immediately caught off guard. And then she proceeded to politely tear me a new one.

She said, "I understand you have some ideas for the show." So I said yes and started man-splaining my position: That I knew what I was talking about and that they could do some things better. That I didn't really like the DJ. That the music needed to be this way and not that way. And all the while, she listened intently, never interrupting.

But then when it was clear I was done, she said, "I appreciate you sharing that."

Yeah, I bet you do, I thought to myself.

That's not what she meant, though.

"Now, we have three other clubs that are beating our door down to have us do the show with them," Leslie said. "And I must tell you that I'm not interested in making any changes. If that doesn't meet with your marketing plan, let me know. We'll take the show to a different club."

Then she stood up, stuck her hand out, and said, "It was great meeting you. I have another meeting to go to." And she walked out.

I honestly had no idea what the hell just happened.

After flying all the way down there and waiting around for her to show up, the whole meeting took less than five minutes. I was stunned! I had never been manhandled by a woman like that in my entire life. And at the time, I had no way to process her reaction.

It's one thing if somebody cusses you out. I can deal with that and know how to respond. But when somebody basically says fuck you without even saying it, and they don't get all bent out of shape? It made my head spin.

Leslie had thoroughly impressed me. Earlier I said this was the moment my life started getting better. It was, but it sure didn't feel like that in the moment, and we wouldn't reconnect until five years later. That must have been the cooling-off time God gave me to get over my grudge. But I had some more growing to do first. I had to hit rock bottom.

16

Like Father, Like Son

Back in Atlanta, it had been nineteen years since I had seen or spoken to my son Jason, and if I'm honest, I really hadn't thought of him that much. It was easier for me not to deal with thoughts like that. When his mother, Dale, and I got divorced just a few months after Jason was born, we went our separate ways and never reached out to each other again. But now, he had tracked me down. And he wanted to meet.

Over the phone, he told me he was still living in West Point, Georgia, and that Dale had kicked him out. I gathered he was now crashing on couches and running out of options, and now that I was finally thinking about the position I had put him in, I felt terrible. I had left him behind and wasn't there for him at all, just like my dad had done to me. I could just imagine how desperate he must feel to be reaching out, since I knew how hard it was for me to do anything like that. I saw a chance to make things right, at least a little bit.

I told Kathy about the call, and although she had always known about Jason, she was just as surprised as I was. "What should I do?" I asked. And after a while, she just said, "Help."

I decided to drive down to meet him, and the whole way down, a crazy tangle of thoughts were running through my head. I was heading toward a reckoning with my own decisions, one I naively thought would never come. Maybe it was a trap and Jason wanted to kick my ass. Maybe he wanted money. Or maybe, like me, he just wanted a dad.

We met at a restaurant and after some awkwardness, we did the only thing we could. We started talking. He said he was trying to get his life together but had pissed his mother off, and she had kicked him out so he had no place to live. I thought back to George and how I didn't feel welcome at home when I was about Jason's age, and the solution seemed obvious.

He actually didn't ask, but I told him he should come live with us in Atlanta and get a new start. At least in the short term, I figured, maybe being around a "loving" family situation would do him some good. I called Kathy and she was on board with the idea, so I headed home to convert our basement into a living space. Jason moved in a few days later.

He was a little sheepish at first, understandably so, but he was helpful around the house and the other kids seemed to like him. Christopher was still in diapers, and Jessica and Justin were in elementary school, but they all got along fine. I knew I couldn't fix everything all at once, but I was glad to give him an opportunity at something new. At that moment in time I felt like I was doing okay as a husband and father, even though I was still hooking up in bars when I travelled and drinking too much. I wanted to help, and I tried to help. But things got weird pretty fast.

Every summer we would take a family vacation, and the year Jason was with us we packed up our Volkswagen van and headed down to Panama City Beach, Florida. A long weekend of relaxing in the sand was just what I needed, and that's what I had my mind set on. But the whole time we were there, I had the strangest sensation. I couldn't put my finger on it, but something was off.

As soon as we arrived, for example, Jason and Kathy went for a long walk on the beach alone. When they got back, she said he just needed a mother's perspective on things with his own mom, which sounded reasonable enough. But they always seemed to be slipping off together and obviously had some inside jokes between them. And then on the way home, the two of them ended up in the van's far back seat.

In the rearview mirror, I noticed Jason laying down with his head in Kathy's lap, and she was stroking his hair and gazing at him lovingly. Now that truly seemed odd. I could understand if it were one of the other kids—one of her kids who were still very young, but Jason was 19.

I didn't get it. But I didn't press, either.

Then one night I had been working late at the club, and after I got home, Kathy and I slipped into bed to have sex. But right in the middle of it all, I glanced over and noticed a red glow coming from under the dresser. What the fuck is that? my suspicious ego screamed.

Before Jason showed up, I had used the basement he was living in as an office. And to make things a little easier, I had bought a set of intercoms from Radio Shack that you plug in to the wall socket. One was in the office and the other was upstairs so I could call up there anytime I needed. But now, for some unknown reason, I could see one under my dresser.

I jumped out of bed in the pitch blackness and went over to check it out, and lo and behold, it was true. There could only be one explanation: Jason must have found the monitors downstairs and put one in our room, and now he was listening in on us whenever he wanted!

I was instantly enraged, but I also had no idea what was going on. Kathy seemed stunned into silence for some reason, so I got dressed and went down to the basement to chew Jason out. It was clear he was eavesdropping on us—he knew I was coming. But I couldn't get an answer as to why.

Did he want to hear us having sex? Was he trying to hear our conversations? He wouldn't give me a straight answer, but at that moment I didn't care as long as he stopped. He promised it would never happen again, and I thought the issue was resolved, so we left it at that. Teenagers do strange things, right?

Then a few weeks later, I got my answer.

After years of working for Richard in the club business, I was finally tired of the late nights and the travel. And although I admired him and was grateful for all he had done for me, professionally and personally, I felt like I had topped out in that career. I wasn't really making much money, either, and along came an offer to get back into the music business as the general manager of a magazine called Hitmakers in Los Angeles.

It was unexpected and I was torn about the decision. I had only been to the West Coast a few times, after all, and was building a life here in Atlanta, but I accepted. I was feeling excited and also a little nervous, and we were just two days from leaving town for good.

There was a ton to do. The moving truck was coming and the house was full of half-packed boxes. We were even having the Volkswagen van shipped, but first I wanted to put some new tires on it. So while I packed, Kathy took Justin and Jessica to school, and after that, she went to the tire shop with Jason and Christopher, who was still just a toddler.

As soon as they left, something Justin had said to me suddenly struck me as odd. I hadn't thought anything of it at the time, but now it was wiggling around in my head like Gene Simmons' god-awful tongue—impossible to ignore.

Like most kids, Justin and Jessica were always scared of thunderstorms. And a few days earlier, Justin had tugged on my hand in that cute, innocent way a young kid does, wanting to let me know that Jason was scared of thunderstorms too. The kids would all get in bed with

Kathy when lightning started flashing—that was always their thing. Now Justin wanted me to know that last time, Jason got in bed too . . . by himself.

I blew it off in the moment. I must have been thinking of something else. But suddenly, that sounded very strange to me. And it also made perfect, terrible sense.

I decided to go downstairs and look through Jason's room, although I have no idea what I expected to find. It was just an instinctive thing, like I needed to check my territory. I poked around aimlessly for a while, then opened up his dresser. I remember grappling with a desperate thought at the same time: Maybe this isn't what it looks like. Maybe Justin was wrong.

I was trying to keep calm, not wanting to acknowledge what might be possible, but right there in the top drawer was the truth: three sets of Kathy's panties, plus two letters they had been writing back and forth. With my adrenaline already spiking, I opened up the first one and could only get through, "I don't know who he thinks he is, but I hate that you have to live with him." And then I lost my mind.

My wife was sleeping with my nineteen-year-old son from another marriage. It was true. There was no denying it. And with everything life had thrown at me up to that point, there was exactly zero chance of me handling it in a healthy way.

Honestly, I don't remember leaving the house. But the next thing I knew I was in my car, hauling ass in rage through the heart of Atlanta. I'm surprised I didn't get pulled over and maybe that says something about Atlanta drivers. Getting stopped right then and there would have been best for everyone. I can only thank God I didn't hurt somebody on the way . . . but then again, my goal was to hurt someone once I got where I was going.

All of the emotional baggage of my childhood had just been dumped out inside my head, and instead of shielding me from the flood, the prideful ego I had built up to contain it made the anger more intense.

What I had discovered was my worst nightmare. Even though I was the one who was always cheating on Kathy, I was terrified of her leaving me. Even back when I was with Jason's mom, I would come home angry every night after imagining her with someone else. It was a big part of the reason we split up. There was just something inside me that was deeply afraid of being rejected, and when I found out Kathy and Jason really were having an affair, it sent me over the edge.

I was on a mission to find the two of them and confront them, and I knew exactly where they were. I plowed into the middle of the tire shop's parking lot action-movie style, with tires screeching and the door open before the car even stopped. But this was no movie. It was broad daylight and a busy little area, full of stores and traffic and people milling around, but my thoughts and vision had both narrowed down to a single bloodthirsty point. I was fully intent on finding Jason, and beating the shit out of him right then and there, and I didn't care who saw it or what the consequences were. I didn't even care if I killed him—that's how deranged I had become. I was stark, raving mad.

The letters were in my hand as I got out of the car, and as soon as I started scanning the crowd of faces, now staring at me in shock, I found Jason's. We locked eyes for just a second and then I saw his gaze fall to my hand, and when he saw the letters, he instantly knew. The confused look on his face turned to sheer terror, and without a word, he sprinted away, running hard and never looking back. He and I both knew he was running for his life.

Kathy knew too. But she had the opposite reaction. She just froze like a statue, the color drained from her cheeks, and her mouth opened in a scream that never came out. If you watch nature documentaries, they talk about the fight, flight or freeze response to a threat, like when a rabbit gets cornered by a fox or something. I walked over and grabbed Kathy by the arm and dragged her to the van, loudly demanding she drive back to the house while I followed in my car with Christopher.

After that very public drama, you'd think my anger would subside, or that maybe I'd start calming down as we drove home. After all, I wasn't exactly faithful to Kathy. But it didn't play out that way.

We got home and I stormed into the house, and instead of talking to Kathy or trying to understand why she did it, I let the anger take over completely. I had been bottling up these feelings of betrayal for so long—my entire life it seemed. And now I could no longer hold back.

I once again flashed back to that day with Bass and the gun and how my mother dragged us into a bedroom to frantically call for help, but I pushed it aside. I didn't want to feel sad. I was so tired of that. I had been pushed around for too long. Now I wanted to feel powerful, like I was in control.

Half of the kitchen was packed up, but the silverware drawer was still full, so I grabbed a butcher knife we got as a wedding present and pointed it at Kathy. "Get down in the basement and start hauling Jason's shit to the road!" I ordered. "We are done with him."

My mind was on fire. It scorched my thoughts and burned me from the inside, starting in my gut and moving out through what seemed like every nerve ending. Kathy went down the stairs and started emptying out Jason's dresser, but she was an emotional wreck and could barely stand. I didn't care. I forced her to take all of Jason's shit up the stairs anyway. My forehead dripped with sweat and I could barely see. But my hands? They were steady. Solid as a rock. And for a moment that honestly scared me.

She was going too slow. I pushed her up against the wall and she dropped a pile of Jason's clothes, so I held the knife to her neck. Her eyes clamped down so tight the tears couldn't escape. Once again she shuddered and pleaded, "I'm sorry." And for a terrible split second I considered killing her. But considered is the wrong word. There was no real decision to make—all I had to do was let go.

17

Rage And Repose

"You brought this on yourself," I fumed, inching closer to oblivion with each breath.

I pressed the knife on Kathy's neck and stared into her closed eyes, every muscle in my body tensed in a physical scream. But really my mind was somewhere else. It was imagining what she had done with Jason. It was thinking back to all the times George had put me down and made me feel worthless. All the times my mother looked at me side-eyed like she didn't want me or talked shit about the father I was never allowed to know. All the times I had caved to addiction. It was like I thought of every single miserable moment of feeling alone on this God-forsaken planet.

Just another flick of the wrist and maybe all that would change. Maybe I'd never feel it again. Maybe she should pay for it all.

I stood there, holding Kathy by the hair and holding my future by a thread. But the moment lingered too long, and the rage began to fade. Then a switch flipped. Something inside me had seen enough. Kathy didn't turn me into this; it wasn't all her fault.

Finally I had a flash of clarity that doused the flames inside me. WHAT THE HELL ARE YOU DOING? my conscious shouted. I let Kathy go and she turned away, sinking to the ground in a heap as I caught my reflection in the mirror. I did not like what I saw. The kitchen light flickered as I held the knife and grimaced in anger. I looked like a monster from a horror movie. And I hated it.

Over and over I just kept thinking, This isn't the way it was supposed to be. I never meant for this to happen. And honestly, that was true. But it was no consolation to Kathy. She might have cheated on me—with my own son, no less—but I had brought this moment on us. I was the one with the knife. I was the one who neglected her needs. I was the one who was always gone. But still, the betrayal smoldered inside me. I was so tired of people disappointing me.

With Kathy still on the floor, I stomped over to the phone and called her sister, Jenny, in Montgomery. I was still mad enough to go off about what a slut her sister was and how she'd probably been sleeping with my son for months now. But Jenny's reaction caught me off guard. I could tell the shock in her voice wasn't genuine. She obviously knew. How could this be? I thought. Was I really that terrible?

I looked at my hands and saw the same white knuckles I saw on Bass all those years ago, and it all came full circle. I forced myself to drop the knife and told Jenny what I had done, and then staggered back in disbelief, slowly walking to the other room. It was like a different world. Only an hour ago I had been packing boxes and thinking of what to do for lunch, and now I didn't even know who I was.

It's not like I hadn't dealt with angry outbursts before—I nearly shot George as a teenager, and almost did the same to Dockery's friend, too—but this was something worse. A lifetime of frustration had exploded like a volcano, and there was nothing I could do to stop it.

Within an hour Jenny and her husband, Robert, rolled in to the driveway with the sheriff's department right behind, and they rushed in to find us both sitting in silence. I was never charged with anything. It was a different time, I guess, and I had cooled off by then. But it was clear I couldn't be around Kathy or the kids. Jenny and Robert took everyone back to Montgomery, and there was just a deafening silence after that. I was alone again.

Two days later I left for California. And I took nothing but my clothes.

———————

The marriage was over, obviously. After Kathy's cheating I might not have wanted to go on anyway, which is crazy considering my personal infidelity. But with the violent rage I just unleashed, there was no chance.

I was not perfect. Far from it, and I knew it. But after five marriages and four children, this was the closest I had gotten to a normal family life. Finding out Kathy was fooling around felt like a dagger in my soul, and I just could not cope with the feeling of abandonment. The fact that it was with my son just made it worse.

I thought back again to what my mother had told me about my father, the one-time war hero I never got to know. I wondered if he had ever done something like this. I wondered if maybe that's why he and my mother really split up, why she hated him so much, and why she seemed to dislike me too. I wondered if I was worse than him.

The anger must have ultimately been some combination of family history, drugs and alcohol, and my complete lack of being equipped to address my problems. But I now think I kept failing so spectacularly at love and lashing out so wildly because I was holding all my feelings inside, and not really letting myself feel them. I would bottle them up and ignore them as the pressure built and built and built until eventually I exploded. I didn't trust anyone enough to confide in, so really, that was my only option.

Plus, I was clearly expecting love to be something it is not.

I expected love to solve all of my problems. It was the one thing I never really had, so I figured it must be the missing ingredient. And when "love" did not live up to that expectation, I became dangerously frustrated.

The sad truth is I don't think I ever loved Kathy, not really. And it was the same with all of the other women I married. The relationships started out physical and were always about what they could do for me. I was basically running around asking everybody, "Hey, do you love me? What can you do for me?" And I wasn't offering anything in return.

To be quite honest, I don't know when Kathy gave up on us and started cheating, because I wasn't paying any attention. I was working all hours of the night, traveling around, cheating constantly and totally consumed by my own needs. I was wrapped up in the club business and drinking and chasing women, and then had the audacity to play the victim when it turned out that Kathy had needs too. But I was a victim too, at least partially. She really had broken the trust I placed in her, whether I deserved to expect it or not.

Over the next few months, we both tried to patch things up for the kids' sake, but it was no use. There was no coming back. It struck me at some point that I was nineteen when I got Dale pregnant, and then Jason was nineteen when he and Kathy got together. Poetic justice I supposed, or just another coincidence in a life I had always suspected was meaningless. Either way, I never saw Jason again, and felt like I had finally, fully become my father.

With no family to lean on, and hardly any true friends, I had nowhere to turn for help. And worse yet, I had just quit working for Richard, the one guy in my life who really had my back. He would gladly have helped me if I knew how to ask, but I had just cut him out of the picture. And I didn't know how to ask anyway. Instead, I kept right on bottling these feelings up.

Alone in every way, I went to Los Angeles needing two things: to lick my wounds and get a fresh start. And with a new job to dive into and nobody who knew me or my past, I could do just that. But I had no idea what was waiting there.

PART 5

The Times They Are A-Changin'

Call to me and I will answer you, and will tell you great and hidden things that you have not known.
Jeremiah 33:3 (ESV)

18

California Dreaming

To get out of a hole, you have to stop digging, and in 1990, I was in deeper than I'd ever been. My fifth marriage had just exploded, and I had chased off my family in a violent rage. Los Angeles was an opportunity to remake myself in any image I wanted, and I intended to take it.

I had always looked at the West Coast and imagined the whole thing was Hollywood. I really am just a small-town Southern boy at heart. So when I arrived, looking to restart my music industry dreams and become someone else, I was half expecting to walk off the plane and into a glitzy new life. And in some ways that was true. In others it was not.

The job my friend had hired me for had me on edge. I had never worked for a music-trade publication before, but I thought I was familiar enough with the concept.

Hitmakers was an industry-specific magazine like the ones I kept track of back when I was in radio—the chart makers like Friday Morning Quarterback or the Gavin Report. They weren't really designed for fans, and I got the job because of my contacts with radio stations back in the Southeast. Honestly, I didn't really understand what my role was going to be, but it sounded cool. And Hitmakers already had a staff in place, so I figured I would learn as I went.

But about two days into the job, I realized the magazine was not really a magazine at all. It was a front for independent record promotion. I was back in the slimy world of payola, and I didn't even mean to be.

Here's how the scam worked. The owners of the magazine already had relationships with big market radio people around the country, and I knew just about everybody in the Southeastern region, so we would use those contacts to set up conference calls. It sounds boring (and it usually was), but it made money.

Each call would generally have a major market music director or program director—somebody who worked in a city like Atlanta or Miami. There would also be one or two medium-sized markets on the call, like a person from Charlotte, North Carolina. And then there would be a small market station too—something like Eclectic, Alabama.

The way we pitched it was we were giving the small market people a chance to be on a call with the major market big shots, and they could benefit from hearing how the big players did things. On the other side, it was the small and medium markets who were breaking new music, so the major market people would get to find out what was reacting around the region.

I probably did fifteen of these calls every week, and eventually, everyone would get around to discussing what songs they were adding to their station. Then we would take that information and basically sell it to the record companies, just like I was doing as an independent promoter years ago. Those companies wanted to know what was working and what wasn't because they had a lot of money invested, and we had the info. But the record companies are not allowed to pay for things like that—that's payola. The whole purpose of our magazine was to create a workaround.

Every issue of the magazine was full of advertisement space that the companies could pay us for. So that's what they did. We would run feature stories about radio insiders like program directors and station owners to make sure they wanted to work with us (everybody wants a big glossy picture of themselves on a magazine cover, right?), and then we sold advertising space to the record companies at really high rates.

It was crazy because if anybody was looking for it, the pay-for-play money would have been obvious. I mean, here's an industry-trade publication that isn't getting a ton of circulation outside of the industry itself, so there's not really any reason to advertise your record company there. Everybody reading the magazine already knows what you have to offer. But they would advertise anyway, and pay a rate far bigger than what it was actually worth.

As soon as I figured that out, my L.A. dream started becoming more of a nightmare. I wasn't truly back in the music business after all. I was just an independent record promoter again, and I wasn't even making the big money.

Ever since I was a kid, I imagined a place where I could become something great, or at least rise above what I already was. I think that was always the motivation behind all the long hours and late nights, and I really did work hard all those years, expecting to be heading toward something. But in L.A., I got very disillusioned, very fast.

I wasn't cut out for that place—so much of the Los Angeles I found turned out to be a facade. Kathy and the kids were originally supposed to move out there with me, so I was living alone in this gigantic house owned by the publisher in Chatsworth, California, and even though it was basically paradise, I couldn't enjoy myself.

The house was a five bedroom ranch with a swimming pool, a hot tub, fruit trees in the yard, and a movie theater in the basement. It even came with some famous neighbors. Roy Rogers had a house up the hillside, where you could look out on the San Fernando Valley below. But I just couldn't make it my own. A year earlier and being a bachelor with an L.A. mansion would have made me feel like I'd died and gone to heaven, but now my life was all out of whack.

Hooking up didn't feel as exciting any more. I wasn't making any friends, since I didn't really fit in. The divorce was being finalized, and this time there were serious legal and money issues concerning the kids. Plus, in this job I was the one giving out the attention, not receiving it, and as we've seen, that isn't really my thing. We were doing under-handed things and I just did not like Los Angeles. It was too big, too spread out. I wasn't the Hollywood type I thought I was.

I kept trudging along until a few months later, when another part of the reason I was hired was revealed.

The owners decided they wanted to start their own radio and records conference—just like the insanely debauched ones I used to attend for the Gavin Report, and they wanted me to set it up. There was still big money to be made in those conferences, and to my bosses, I was the per-fect person for the job. I had taken part in them before, and I knew all of the radio and record label people who would need to be invited. Plus, I had a background in advertising and hotel operation from working for Richard all those years.

It was the same setup as the others. We would book a hotel for one rate and then charge the record companies another, and whatever happened inside those suites was none of our business. I was just at the point where I didn't really care anymore.

And then out of the blue, she showed up.

Following our meeting five years earlier—the one where she skillfully put me in my place without even breaking a sweat—Leslie and I hardly had any contact. There wasn't any bad blood or anything. We just didn't have a reason to be in touch. But in L.A., she was one of the radio people I would set up conference calls with. She never had any idea what we were really using them for, of course—nobody did. For her it was just an opportunity to share perspectives with other radio pros, and during those calls we acknowledged that we knew each other, but we didn't really get into it . . . thank God.

Then, as I was setting up the first Hitmakers magazine conference in Birmingham, the yearly Gavin Report event in San Francisco started up, and I went to check out the competition in more detail.

I was at my peak as a jaded Hollywood hipster, looking sullen and decked out in my black jeans, black jean jacket, T-shirt, and long hair pulled back in a pony tail. Really putting out a vibe that I was too cool for any of this stuff. I checked into the hotel and dropped off my bag, then came back down to the lobby to get a drink. And as I walked off the elevator I heard a soft, playful voice say, "Lanny . . . West."

19

And Along Came LuLu

In the moment just before those words, I was flat broke emotionally. Didn't have a single dollar in the bank. I was literally dragging my soul through every day. Five marriages down, no spiritual or moral compass, and a longstanding reliance on booze just to get by. But as I turned around and saw Leslie Fram—the first time we had seen each other in person since that disastrous meeting five years earlier—I smiled for the first time in about a year.

Without ever really talking about it, we hung out the whole weekend of that convention. It felt great and also incredibly strange to me, since it was the first time in my life I was around a woman without trying to get in bed with her. Not because she wasn't attractive—she was beautiful with dark hair, kind eyes, and a slim figure I was magnetically drawn to. Plus, she had the put-together confidence of a woman who knew herself and wasn't susceptible to anybody's bullshit, which I knew about first-hand.

Normally, that would put me off, but something had changed inside me. I was like an old turn table with a new needle. She had this energy that was consuming and fulfilling at the same time. I felt a weight lift off of me. She was special.

I spent the whole weekend with her attending conference events and sharing meals, and we even went to see our first concert together, a band called Jellyfish that was part of the convention. It was as close to perfect as I can think of, and I felt so alive—maybe for the first time in my life.

The last night we were there, we just sat at the bar talking with two of her friends until about three in the morning. She didn't drink much. Although I did, like an idiot. But at some point I remember excusing myself and thinking, There's something here. I can't explain it, but I can feel it.

With Leslie, I could have a conversation and talk about things on a deeper level. I didn't have to put up a front or boast. She just seemed to get me. I wasn't with the other women I hung around with for their intellect; my attraction to them was purely sexual. I always thought that was just the way love started. But this was different.

I didn't want to get my hopes up, but secretly I was thinking, Maybe this is who I've been looking for all my life.

The next day, Leslie went back to her job, which was now in Atlanta at the radio station Power99, and I went back to L.A. But in my heart I was still with her. I sent her flowers once we got settled, and that was something I had definitely never done before. I'd never even thought to do it before. I was like a different person.

We started having phone conversations on a daily basis and I told her about some of my past. It was hard and didn't happen all at once, but we were just friends at that point, and she didn't judge me. She tried to help, like she always does even to this day. And eventually, a relationship started emerging.

Even though I had really strong feelings, I think I was a bit afraid of what they meant. I held back and didn't ask her what she felt about me, probably for fear of getting disappointed. But even that was a good sign.

Normally, I would rush headlong into a relationship and we would get married a few months later, but that was all about me "sealing the deal." This time, though, I actually cared about what Leslie thought and wanted.

———————

After a few months, I had to put a Hitmakers conference together in Atlanta, and I knew I would see her. It was incredibly nerve-racking. My heart was racing for a week leading up to it.

At that time, Leslie was the assistant program director and co-host of the morning show at Power99, so the day I arrived in Atlanta, I tuned in to listen. She and her partners were interviewing Kevin Costner. It was just a couple of years after the movie Bull Durham came out, so at the end of the interview she teed Mr. Costner up to deliver one of the movie's most famous lines.

They were saying their goodbyes and she said something like, "One last thing before you go. I've always wondered, how do you like your kisses?" And without missing a beat the Hollywood star fired back, "Well, Leslie, I believe in long, slow, deep, soft, wet kisses that last three days." She was a pro. I didn't think I could be any more impressed by her, but I was.

Fast-forward to later in the day, and I had asked Leslie if we could use her office for the weekly Hitmakers conference call. I told her that I really liked the morning show, especially her interview with Costner. Then we got everybody on the line and as we're sitting there discussing playlists, I noticed she was writing on a notepad. This stuff was not anywhere near interesting enough to be taking notes about.

She finished up and slid the note over to me. It said, "How do you like your kisses?"

Once again she had stunned me into silence. This time, just as I was supposed to pick up the conversation on the call. She giggled at me as the awkward pause lingered, and I finally stuttered back to life, smiling like a bandit the whole time.

This really was my dream woman. She had my number without a doubt, and even did me the favor of making the first move. She swore that she had never done anything like that before, but I was thinking she'd never need to again, because I was hers in that instant.

Later that night, she showed up late to a fancy dinner for the conference planning meeting I had put together and turned everybody's head by walking in wearing this attention grabbing peach-colored pantsuit. But instead of saying hello to all the big wigs, she came straight over to me and whispered, "So, I guess I'm your date tonight."

I was over the moon. We spent the evening together laughing and not really presenting ourselves as a couple, but trying it on for size. It just felt right. We even took several people dancing at America Pie, and afterwards, I walked her to her room. But nothing happened. I did the gentlemanly thing and thanked her for a wonderful night and meant every word.

I was already feeling like this relationship was meant to be, but it's funny looking back, because I can see God didn't trust me to figure it out. Judging by my track record, He had every right.

20

Coming Home

I'd just had the most wonderful evening of my life with Leslie, and I could already tell there was something different about this relationship. It felt like everything I never knew I wanted. But it was still just casual dating, and we were long distance. I woke up the next morning to a call from my old boss Richard. It turned out he wanted me to come back and take over American Pie again.

He was downright desperate, apparently, because this time he was willing to give me a small stake in part ownership of the damn thing. I guess things had not gone well while I was gone, and it hadn't even been a full year yet. I was a handful and I knew it, but I also knew I made Richard a shitload of money . . . and he knew it too.

I accepted Richard's offer on the spot. He actually made a bad deal because I would have taken a job doing dishes, and it wasn't just because I was ready to leave L.A. For the first time in my life, I wanted to dedicate myself to something other than me—someone other than me.

After I told Leslie I was moving back and would be able to see her more often, I flew back to L.A. and put in my notice at Hitmakers. And it felt better than any drug I'd ever taken.

———

I flew back to Atlanta on June 18, 1991, and the next night Leslie and I had our first official date. I took her to my favorite Chinese restaurant and had even put together a mix tape of what were probably the most ridiculously cheesy (but oh, so romantic) songs ever made. I wish we still had that tape. It was my version of the Say Anything scene with John Cusack.

Not a day went by that we didn't go out, and sometimes we would both attend dinners with record label people and things like that, but nobody knew we were dating. We were seen together all the time, but since I was spending a ton of money advertising American Pie on Power99—which was going on before I even came back and had nothing to do with us—it was easy to keep under wraps.

Of course, being terrified of ruining what we had and having no idea how to do things the right way, I kept telling Leslie I liked everything the way it was. It was quite a while before anything physical happened between us, and that fact was even shocking to me since it was not how I normally did things.

Throughout this book, I've hardly talked at all about what my wives were like as people, and that's not really because of bias. I just never got to know them. We never really shared anything about ourselves and really never had anything in common. But here was this person who I just wanted to be with.

I loved hanging out with her and talking. I could be myself and didn't need to put up a front. I loved getting to know her. I had completely stopped doing cocaine and it wasn't even a conscious decision. I was just busy and didn't need it. And although my drinking was still heavy, even Richard could tell I was a profoundly changed man. I would say my only regret is that it took me so long to get to that place. But if it had happened any sooner, I might not have met Leslie.

Those months through the end of 1991 and into 1992 were a happy blur for me. Leslie and I were lost in each other and doing well professionally. I would argue she even had a hand in the rise of alternative rock, since 99X, which Power99 rebranded as in 1992, was one of the premiere radio stations to begin playing it around this time.

The seasons changed and March came around. Just for a little background, I'm the kind of guy who would throw myself a "surprise" birthday party. That's because I loved parties, but also because no one in my life ever threw them for me. And they were usually awesome.

This year there was no party but I didn't mind since I had Leslie to be with and we had plans for a nice dinner. But just before we left she said, "Look, when we get done with dinner, there's a family who lives across the hall from my apartment, and they have twin boys who are also celebrating a birthday today and they are huge 99X fans. They're having a party in the clubhouse and asked if I would stop by. Do you mind?"

I was like "Sure, of course!" I thought nothing of it, and we went to our favorite restaurant, Chow in Virginia Highlands.

For the life of me, I still have no idea what came over me that night. But we were close to the end of dinner, and it was one of those slow meals where you had plenty of time to talk between courses. It was great. But what I'm about to write here is exactly how it happened. And after reading it, you'll know exactly how long it took.

I said "Leslie, I want to ask you a question. What would you think about spending the rest of your life with me?" And she goes "Yes. Can I get a check?" And flags down a waitress.

I just sort of looked around, stunned again as usual, unsure of what the hell had just happened!

She did know I had just proposed marriage, right? Granted, even I didn't know I was going to do it, but it was pretty clear. I was starting to get a little worried, but as we left the restaurant I could tell she heard me loud and clear.

What I didn't know was that the party for those kids across the hall was actually a surprise party for me at the apartment club house, and we were late. There was no time to make a big deal of it, and apparently, she had already made up her mind!

We went to the party, and it was grand in every way. She had invited all kinds of friends I had made over the years, and we reveled in the joy of our secret. At first we didn't tell anyone, and we would just share a loving glance across the room or I would tug on her finger, right where the ring would go.

I had been a fiancé five times before this, but it had never felt even remotely this good. Life was perfect. At the end of the night we told two of our closest friends about our news and went to sleep in each other's arms.

———————

I was more excited to marry Leslie than I was for any other moment in my life, but it was kind of a private joy for me. I didn't bother telling my family about us. My mother and I had a falling out during a visit while I was married to Kathy, and we hadn't seen each other since.

No, my family would not be attending our wedding. But Leslie's family was a different story. She had a happy childhood growing up in Fairhope, Alabama, and out of respect for her mom and dad wanted to have a nice church wedding. I still wasn't religious, but was all for it. Whatever made her happy.

But as typically happens, a lot of people other than Leslie and I, started speaking into the details. They thought it should be at this church or that church and on this day or at least not that day, because Auburn would play Alabama in the yearly Iron Bowl. Seriously? We don't even watch football.

It was really weighing on Leslie until one rainy night at my place. It was coming down like cats and dogs. As I was cooking, I saw her car pull up outside, but she didn't come in for about forty-five minutes. Dinner was totally cold and I was a bit disappointed at first, but it turns out she was talking to her mom.

Leslie's mom was one of the greatest women ever, and she and Leslie's dad became family to me—they were the mom and dad I never had. But planning the wedding was getting really difficult. Apparently they had hashed it out during that call, though, because at the end of it her mom said, and I quote, "Just go fucking get married." You would have had to know Adel to appreciate that response.

I was ecstatic. That was on a Sunday, so on Monday I found a retired Air Force chaplain and set up the wedding for that Friday. Leslie's sister and her husband, Don, and their boy, Steven, came up. Plus, my three youngest children were with us, and we showed up at this chaplain's house with smiles all around. But when we knocked on the door, an older gentleman came out to greet us and said, "So where's Lulu?"

In my mind, I was thinking I had messed up again, so I said, "Uh, sir? I'm sorry but there's nobody named Lulu here." He just kind of smiled and said, "Well, I wrote it down right here," and showed me a piece of paper. The way he wrote Leslie looked like "Lulu," so that's been her nickname ever since.

We got married in a short-but-happy little ceremony and went right from there to a BBQ joint nearby, and that's probably where our fetish for BBQ comes from, which still lasts today. Then we hopped a flight to Jamaica for our honeymoon, and when we came home, all of our friends in the music industry threw us a huge reception at the Ritz Carlton. There we were, off and running, never to look back.

It had been less than a year since I returned to Atlanta, but my entire life and personality had changed. I was truly in love and genuinely felt like I knew what that meant, and it was exciting. I had found my soul mate.

From the moment I began seeing her, I've never even come close to thinking of another woman. My drinking kept up and it did cause some problems for us, but all the cheating stopped. The cocaine use stopped. And I've never gotten angry at Leslie like I did in the past. Probably because this relationship wasn't all about me getting what I wanted. It was about showing and giving love back to her. I was not going to do anything to destroy this relationship, and the more we were together, the more that feeling grew.

Looking back now at all the turning points, all the things that happened, God was there trying to get my attention. Now He finally had it, but He wasn't done with me yet.

21

Big Changes

My personal life was finally in a positive place, but work-life balance was still an issue. American Pie was open from 11 a.m. to 4 a.m. seven days a week, and I was committed to that. When I do things, I tend to do them to the extreme, and I was getting to the point where I was burnt out.

I love Richard to death. For all of my faults, he saw something in me and kept giving me opportunities to succeed, and I felt a need to prove myself. The club made a lot of money and ran smoothly when I was in charge, and we were always running wild promotions to keep people coming back. We were advertising on 99X, which was an alternative rock station, but somehow had great success promoting these kooky shows that had nothing to do with that scene.

We'd bring in oldies bands like The Tams or Chairmen of the Board, and people would show up to dance the shag all night. And one night we fenced off the whole property and brought a circus tent in for KC and the Sunshine Band, pulling in over $160,000. The commercials we ran were ridiculous and caught people's attention, so maybe they showed up for the irony of it all.

But really, I was just going back to my old playbook from my radio days, and it felt pretty easy. One time we even revisited the infamous Jello Jump stunt. We called it the Great Power Plop, and it was a true triumph.

Just like the old days, I got American Pie tied in with a local dairy. They would supply all kinds of silly, milk-related giveaways to 99X—things like Milk Duds, chocolate milk, milk of magnesia. People would call in to the morning show to answer trivia questions. If they guessed right, they went into the winners' pool, and from there we selected twelve people for the event.

Meanwhile, we put up a huge tent in the parking lot of American Pie and basically built a pasture under it, complete with a big grassy area lined by hay bales. Then we brought out the dairy's mascot, a real live Holstein. Twelve squares were marked out on the grass—one for each contestant—and everybody got a number. Before the event we had also partnered with a local Ford dealership, and the idea was whichever square the cow took a dump in, that person won a Ford Mustang for a year. That's a little better than the stereo we gave away back in Montgomery.

In the end, there were about six hundred people standing around in a parking lot, drinking and eating, and ultimately, waiting four hours for a cow to take a shit. What a world.

Stuff like that made American Pie legendary, and being behind it all fed my ego. But I expected just as much from the staff as I did of myself and that tended to create friction.

Ever since I got married, I didn't party or hang out with the staff anymore, and we started drifting apart. I never reprimanded or interviewed a waitress without someone else being in the office, so no one could accuse me of being inappropriate. Everything I did was fair and above board, but I wasn't always the most compassionate.

The staff would complain to Richard, and for a couple of years, we were in this cycle where I would get fired, only to be brought back to clean things up six months later when the staff started stealing from the registers or the waitresses got caught doing drugs during their shifts or one of the managers got caught having sex with a waitress in the beer cooler.

After the fourth time I got fired, I decided not to come back. It was 1995 and I had gotten to know a guy named Mike who ran a small booking agency. It turned out he was working with this college-town band called Memory Dean who needed management help. We worked as partners for a while until Mike and the band fell out, and all of a sudden, I was a full-blown artist manager. Since it was just me, I came up with the name JustWest Entertainment. I was pretty good at thinking up names.

Management was fun for me. I liked finding talented artists and listening to their dreams, and I liked working with them to get there. I think I was good at anticipating needs and I had good connections in both the record label community and at radio. So over twenty years I was able to help a lot of acts get off the ground.

But on the flip side of that, management is an all-or-nothing kind of business. Until you score a hit, it can be a lonely lifestyle filled with constant problems that need attention. And it also doesn't pay jack at the lower levels because the fees are typically a percentage of what the artist makes.

Nevertheless, I helped quite a few artists get record deals and build up a presence on the radio, and got to watch as their audiences grew. Rock bands like Memory Dean, but also the indie-folk duo 22 Brides, singer-songwriter Sonia Leigh, and also Matthew Perryman Jones, who really could have been a Grammy winner in my opinion.

The only problem was that none of the bands made it really big, and I struggled with that for twenty years. They saw success on their own terms and got to do what they loved for a living, which is what most will tell you is the real goal, but I took it as a personal failure in a lot of cases.

I think I made it that way because instead of just focusing purely on the business aspect, I always ended up being friends with these people. The most successful managers often have a reputation of being ruthless, and in a lot of ways, that stereotype is true—just because it kind of has to be. Otherwise, they'd be managers like me who you've never heard of.

But it stuck with me over the years and took me a long time to work through. I kept seeing people who didn't have near the expertise or connections that I had calling themselves managers, and their bands, which I thought were less talented than mine, kept getting big breaks. I felt that my competitors were all failing upward and I just couldn't get it to happen, so it started me down a road of once again being angry all the time.

Actually, I was frustrated and jealous. I still craved the prestige of an important station in life. And even though I knew how to love Leslie, I still didn't know how to love myself.

Still, I'll never forget my time as an artist manager. Over the years, we did tours in Europe where the crowds were so in love with my guy they fed him shots until Leslie and I had to literally carry him back to a hotel—and he was just the opening act. The headliner was pissed.

Other times I'd take on a client and find out that even though they were capable of making six figures a year on movie and tv sync licensing alone, they couldn't follow through with a simple promise to their own fans and had debts so large they needed to live with you and your wife.

Sometimes I look back and laugh, like about how we turned a tour van into a mobile breast milk-pumping station for a band with two new mothers in it. And other times it was frustrating and heartbreaking, like when one band scored an opening slot at Atlanta's massive Midtown Music festival, absolutely rocked ten thousand potential fans and landed on the front of the city's newspaper, only to get drunk backstage and offend the staff so badly they were effectively blacklisted.

For every step forward in management there seemed to be two steps back, and that's tough for a guy who tends to look for love in his job. Quite frankly, artist management is one of the most thankless jobs out there. When things are going great it's because the band is "so special," and when things are bad, it's because the manager is shit.

But I liked working for myself, and I've been doing it ever since. Plus, it allowed me to work from anywhere, which meant I was able to take care of Leslie's parents as they neared the end of their lives. Five years into my management career, I moved to Fairhope so I could help care for them while she stayed in Atlanta full time. After never truly feeling like I had a mother or father—at least ones who cared for me unconditionally—they had become my surrogate parents.

Fairhope is a quaint little Gulf of Mexico town on the eastern shore of Mobile Bay, a real heaven on Earth and the exact opposite of Atlanta's hustle and bustle. I cherished the time I got to spend with her parents. It was tricky business, though.

Leslie's mother, Adel, had contracted Hepatitis C from a knee surgery long ago, and all of a sudden, it raised its ugly head. The disease prevents your body from filtering out ammonia properly, and if it's not monitored very carefully, the ammonia will build up and impact brain function, which eventually leads to death. We had to be very careful about her protein and salt intake, so I was with them pretty much constantly. And on top of that, I was managing bands across the country.

Her father, Joe, was an ex-Marine, and he was truly a man's man. When Leslie was a kid, he and Adel owned a little neighborhood grocery store with the family house on the same property, and the stories they told about that place were amazing to me.

Joe was a master carpenter and they were well-known and loved in the community. Leslie told me that every Sunday she and her siblings got to invite friends over, and they would sit around and play guitar while Mr. Fram cooked for them on the brick grill he had built. It was this completely foreign world that I knew nothing about, and it honestly made me very emotional.

For any kid who grows up in a less-than-happy home, I think you subconsciously start to hate those families who are happy. It eventually colors the way you look at people in general and your whole world view, and I came to realize I'd been holding on to that a long time. But there was nothing to hate about this family. I had wasted so much time on that already.

Leslie's parents were also very understanding people—another foreign concept of parenting to me. When she and I got engaged, I wanted to do the right thing for once, so I made plans to go down to Fairhope and ask Joe for her hand in marriage, and it was scarier than I had imagined. They knew I had been married before, but they didn't know the extent of it all. But Joe surprised me.

We got down there and everybody took a seat on the sofa. I had been rehearsing what to say in my head for days on end. I could just feel my legs shaking and was fighting the urge to sprint out the door with every heartbeat, but I really wanted to do this.

We chatted a bit, and finally, I worked up the courage. But just as I took a big breath and looked over at Leslie, she suddenly jumped up and excused herself to visit her sister down the block! Daddy's girl didn't want to be there if a murder was about to occur.

It was cute, although it didn't make what I had to say any easier. This guy was a six-foot-four ex-Marine and I was a skinny ex-coke head. But they were gracious and patient, and all went well. I was able to convince him that I had turned a corner and that I truly loved Leslie more than anything in the world. And it was pretty easy, since it was true.

Over those three years, I took over a lot of the things Mr. Fram would do to keep up the property, and I learned things from him about skilled work—stuff I had never even come into contact with through my step-fathers.

He had a garage full of tools and even in his old age, he put them to use, so I learned how do lots of basic carpentry and even some concrete work. It's come in handy since then and would have long ago as well, if I had known to seek it out. I'm not a sports guy, but we would watch a game together every afternoon and have these long, rambling conversations about all kinds of things.

It felt like I had become part of the family and like I had gone back in time about thirty years in some ways. Then there was Adel, who had one of the greatest, most infectious laughs I've ever heard. Eventually, I really did consider them as my mother and father, and it was a great feeling to experience. I can only imagine what I would have turned out like if they had been my parents. I probably wouldn't have been so desperate to "be somebody" in my work, and I probably would have been more deliberate with my relationships. And I probably would have been a better parent to my own kids too.

I didn't take care of Joe and Adel because anybody asked me to—even Leslie never did that. I did it because I wanted to and because I loved them. But it was a short time that I got to know them, from just before Leslie and I got married until 2003 when Adel passed. Joe followed her along a few years later. That time was very important to me. I finally knew what I had missed out on in my childhood, and that made me sad. But it made me grateful too. They had changed my perspective, just like Leslie did, but in their own way.

One of the great things I'll never forget was getting ready to go to Adel's funeral. I hadn't shaved in several days, and Mr. Fram was very clean cut, always groomed up in the Marine Corp way. I'm a little over six feet tall, but even at that point he was taller than me, and before we left the house, he walked up to me in a hallway.

There was no anger or disappointment in his voice, but he stopped and looked down a little to meet my eyes and said, "Is there a reason you haven't shaved today?" I sort of stammered a little, and then immediately went and shaved. Family was a thing to be respected.

22

The Tale Of Liver Boy

Just before Adel passed, I had a mysterious health scare of my own. It was unlike anything I have ever experienced—before or since—and it changed my life forever. I was already on my way to becoming a different person, but this was like God giving me a nudge.

It all started with a bad fever on May 19, 2003. And when I say bad, I mean 104.2. I couldn't sleep it off and the sweats and aches were unbearable, so I called the doctor and went in for some help. Help was hard to come by, though. One doctor after another was stumped by my condition.

At first they suspected pneumonia, but when X-rays came back negative the diagnosis moved to a possible viral infection. Alright, I thought, what do I do for that? Well, nothing really. You can't use antibiotics on a virus, so it would have to run its course.

I went home. But by May 25, I couldn't take it anymore and checked myself into the emergency room, still battling a high temperature but now constant headaches as well. This time the doctor called in an infectious-disease specialist. They did some blood work and felt I possibly had a serious viral infection called cytomegalovirus (CMV), which of course, there was no treatment for it.

They sent me home again but nothing changed. So before long I was back at the doctor's office for another round of blood work. By now

I had elevated liver enzymes and a white-blood-cell count of around 19,000, which the doctor said was way too high. It should have been between 4,500 and 11,000, and that meant my immune system was ramping up to fight something off. They ordered up an ultrasound, since I was also now experiencing major pain in my abdomen, too, and it did not reveal good news.

There was something on my liver, but they weren't sure what, so the next step was a CT scan and a biopsy of some possible cysts. I was getting nervous now, but the doctors were still acting very calm. When they learned Leslie and I had recently been to the Dominican Republic, though? Then they got worried.

———

What's wrong with the Dominican Republic, you ask? Well, it meant I might have a nasty little parasite called echinococcus, a disease-spewing worm that literally eats you from the inside and causes cysts in the liver, brain, pancreas, and lungs. They don't put those in the brochure.

I needed more blood work to see if that was the case, but unfortunately the only lab that could test for this thing was in Los Angeles, and it would take up to ten days to get the results. We couldn't do anything until then because if I had the parasite, and the doctor nicked one of those cysts during the biopsy, it would kill me. But after a few days, I didn't care.

Waves of pain radiated through my head and abdomen. It felt like my brain was getting pushed out my ears, and I was pretty well convinced that little worm really was in there, putting cysts on my brain. The fever just would not go down, and at this point, the doctors were also convinced of the parasite—even without the lab results—so they started me on antibiotics right away. I had a feeling this was a bad sign, since I'd never heard of a doctor skipping steps like that.

The numbers kept getting worse. On June 9, my white-blood-cell count was 31,000, and the next morning it was up to 59,000. My whole body was going to war!

Then on June 12, the lab results finally came back . . . negative for the deadly Caribbean parasite. Obviously I was relieved to hear that, but after doing the long-delayed biopsy, I got some more bad news.

There was a cantaloupe-sized spot on my liver that was severely abscessed. It would need to be removed. I was really regretting all those drinking binges. Maybe this was my punishment.

———————

Ultimately, a surgeon removed 26 percent of my liver, pulling it out through a twelve-inch incision on my right side. I spent three days in intensive care but the fever finally broke, and mercifully, I started healing.

I finally went home on June 23, just over a month after the ordeal began, and because of how bad the abscess was, they estimated my recovery would take a year. It ended up being closer to two, actually, but the upside was that for the first time in my life, I was living right.

I didn't touch a drop of alcohol that whole time. I ate healthy. And I really focused on getting well. As soon as I was out of the woods the drinks started flowing again, of course, even worse than before in some ways. But it opened a new area of interest in my life. One which would come into play later on.

23

Headed North

The craziest part of my whole health scare was this: the doctors never could figure out what caused it. In the end I had forty-two blood tests, eight CT scans, an ultrasound, an MRI, a colonoscopy, a biopsy, and lost a huge chunk of my liver along with forty-five pounds. But at least I was alive. It was the most agonizing two months of my life by far.

The best guess is that when they started me on antibiotics to treat for the possible parasite, those drugs may have killed whatever germ was responsible. But with how things turned out in the years that followed, I think a higher power may just as likely have been involved.

Following my surgery and during my two-year recovery period, Leslie and I rode out wave after wave of change. Our lives changed drastically, so maybe the liver disease was just to toughen me up.

First, the radio station Leslie had helped become a major piece of public life in Atlanta—not to mention a legend in music history—was sold off by its corporate owners. Even though 99X had helped kick-start the alternative rock movement in the '90s, arguably launching the careers of huge bands like Matchbox Twenty, The Foo Fighters, and The Smashing Pumpkins, that era was done and over as far as the new owners were concerned. NuMetal was in, and bands like Limp Bizkit, Creed, and Disturbed would be the next Beatles . . . or something like that.

They cleaned house and changed almost everything so Leslie was out of a job, but she took it in stride. We knew something else would come along, and we were right.

I was working with the artist Sonia Leigh at the time and during a trip to meet with some Nashville publishers, Leslie got a call. In typical fashion, she had spent her time off helping to get her former team members at 99X new jobs, and a few of them had landed in New York City. Leslie had been in touch with a station's general manager there to make sure this happened, and he knew her work. He had been at the company that owned 99X while Leslie was program director.

It wasn't just that she had a great reputation as a morning show host, which she did. She was also an excellent manager with a knack for building extremely effective teams. I think it's because she's a great judge of character, and also because she picks people who are passionate about the thing at the core of their job—in radio, that's music. It sounds like a given, but you might be surprised how many musically ambivalent people work in radio.

The New York station was about to switch formats from jazz to a classic/alternative-rock hybrid, and the GM wanted her to be the new program director and morning show co-host with Matt Pinfield, former 120 Minutes V-Jay on MTV. So on the drive to Nashville, she said, "Yes."

Neither one of us had ever thought of living in New York City, and it scared me to death. I would go up there occasionally for events, but I never once took the subway on those trips. It just seemed like a good place to get killed in a hundred different ways.

The move was a big leap of faith, but we took it as a couple, found a great 650-square-foot apartment just off Wall Street, learned the subway system, explored many great restaurants, took in the sights, and grew to really love the Big Apple.

We would walk seven or eight miles every Sunday just exploring the city, and there was so much to do and see that I never imagined. You can't get a sense of the New York community by visiting. You have to be immersed in it, and that is a much different view that just seeing the typical big-city issues of crime and poverty that I thought of before. I came to see why many people refuse to live anywhere else—and for a heavy drinker, there's nothing better than a city that lets you get liquor delivered to your apartment.

It was a time of firsts and changing perceptions all around. Personally, I had recovered from the liver surgery and was back on the bottle, but I had made some major changes in my life, especially around food and nutrition. After a lifetime of not really thinking about what I was putting in my body, I discovered that I had celiac disease and started getting really serious about the fuel I was burning. I was reading and researching, and eventually got to the point where I was eating sugar-free, gluten-free, and dairy-free, and I had never felt better.

Eating healthy is tied in with mental well-being, I think. If you're not in a good headspace, it's pretty hard to care about quality food. You're mostly looking for another way to escape, and eating is just another way to do it. I had always been thin but not healthy, but now I was happy enough to try and do something good for myself. It was all because of Leslie, and meanwhile, she was at her new radio station doing exactly what she had done in Atlanta.

She put a team of people together who were real music aficionados, and the salespeople were shocked. When we arrived it was clear they didn't think this little Southern girl knew enough about New York to make anything happen, but she and her team took a station which was effectively nonexistent before she arrived, to massive ratings with universal name recognition across one of the biggest, most diverse cities on the planet—all while doing a popular morning show. She hates it when I say it, but back then, she was one of the most powerful women in the radio industry. And soon she would get even more influential.

We moved to New York in 2008, and by 2011 things were undoubtably going great for Leslie professionally. I was still managing bands and would fly back and forth to Atlanta a few times a month, where we kept our house as a home base for my artists. But things can change fast in the corporate world, and that year Leslie's station was part of a big buyout. The problem was, the company that bought this huge portfolio of radio stations couldn't afford them all, so they immediately dumped some, including Leslie's.

Right away, she got an offered a job with CBS to take over programming at their San Francisco station, Live105, but I'm glad she held off on accepting that one. Leslie had kept in contact with her old boss from Atlanta, a guy named Brian Phillips, and he was now working in Nashville as the president of CMT. They had sort of a mentor relationship, and his point to Leslie was that she had gone about as far as was possible in radio. Maybe it was time to try a different industry? He had a plan in mind, I think, a very crafty plan.

Leslie interviewed with some record labels and satellite radio services, and then Brian suggested "Hey, why not meet with some people at Viacom?" (Viacom owns CMT, MTV and VH1 and is based in New York). His plan, unbeknownst to us, was for Leslie to be CMT's senior vice president of music strategy. But he needed his bosses to meet her first, so they would sign off on bringing in someone from outside TV broadcasting. They loved her, of course, and the next day he offered her the job.

There we were in New York City, and we had taken a huge leap of faith just to get there three years earlier. Now there was another big leap to make, since alternative radio was the only home Leslie had ever known. She was going to plunge into a whole new career path, and we were heading to a new city once again. But we were doing it together.

We found a house and sold the place in Atlanta, and Leslie's first day at CMT was September 1, 2011. Even then I felt one step closer to something, but I couldn't put my finger on it. I was just happy that we were together and healthy, and that Leslie was being so appreciated as the amazing person she was. That thought itself made me feel good, because I knew how far I had already come.

If the same thing were happening to one of my previous wives, I probably would have been jealous and found some way to sabotage the whole deal. But this former alternative rocker has been fully embraced by the country music industry.

Brian's intent was to bring Leslie to Nashville because she knows how to build a team and build relationships. Those things are both important and she's done well with them, but there's more to her success. She's got a strong sense of justice and is not content to just go along with the flow—she's the perfect person to change things from the inside.

Since 2011, Leslie's become a central figure in country music, even though the cable television model that CMT relied on when she got there was already fading out. CMT was really in danger of going under, washed over by the tide of streaming TV and digital music. But Leslie and her teams have created these huge initiatives that not only keep the brand relevant, but also do real positive work for country music—things like the Next Women of Country series and the Equal Play initiative, which both address a lack of opportunity for female artists in country. She's revitalized the whole brand's voice, just like she revitalized me.

PART 6

Humble and Kind

He drew me up from the pit of destruction, out of the miry bog, and set my feet upon a rock, making my steps secure. He put a new song in my mouth, a song of praise to our God. Many will see and fear, and put their trust in the LORD.
Psalm 40:2-3 (ESV)

24

Getting Curious

Nashville was the start of a new adventure for us, but it was also the end of some things for me. After we arrived, I made the decision to stop managing artists altogether. I had already stopped working with the ones in New York and just wasn't going to mess with it anymore.

I was tired of the work, and as I said earlier, it is the most thankless career on the planet. It was like babysitting grown adults or trying to get a teenager to do their homework, and too often the work was in vain. Leslie was regularly asking me why I wanted to continue in this field and now I started asking myself the same question. But more importantly, I came to the realization that over all the years of my life and all the things I had done, I didn't even know who I was.

I had spent so much time pursuing things that would build me up or make me feel different—things like status, drinking, drugs, and sex that I had no idea who Lanny actually was beyond what I did for a living, or even what I did for fun. It was a scary revelation because my whole life, a big part of my confident persona was knowing exactly who I was and what I was about, and not giving a shit about the B.S. the world said I should care about. I was so sure. But the longer I was with Leslie, the more I was realizing it was a lie.

Deep down I was angry all the time, most likely fueled by my drinking and lack of what I viewed as success. I was trying to run from things that hurt too much to think about. I was trying to escape my past and prove

I was above it, and to do that, I put on all these different masks, hoping I wouldn't be recognized for the broken man I was. And it worked. Nobody recognized Lanny. Not even me.

After more than fifty years of working in the entertainment industry and living a life of indulgence and excess, I was near a physical and mental breakdown. My energy and the spirit I always felt like I had even in tough times was being sucked out of me more and more each day by an industry that's designed to chew people up and spit them out—then grab another person and do it to them. It's not a sustainable way to live, just throwing more and more beautiful and creative kids into this machine and watching them come out defeated and dejected on the other side.

I had been keeping this feeling hidden pretty well, but I knew that if I didn't make some serious changes, I was going to snap. And from past experience, I knew it would not be pretty.

When I finally cut ties with my final artist, the music business dream I started chasing at my high school radio station was officially dead. And honestly, it was a huge load off of my shoulders, even though I was still owed over $160,000 from my clients over the years—money I knew I would never collect.

I think now that on balance, my twenty years of artist management were not unsuccessful because I was a bad manager or because the bands were bad. Looking back, I feel that God never intended for me to stay in that business, so He made it a struggle. It just took me twenty years to figure it out.

Now that I was free of that struggle, I could finally get serious about figuring out who Lanny was. I had survived a terrible childhood, years and years of drug use and sexual addiction, an anger problem that threatened me and everyone around me, and a health scare that could have killed me. And although I was still drinking a lot, it was time to start the process of self-discovery and emotional healing. But to do that, I needed to redirect my energy into something I loved. I just had no idea what it would be.

When you spend a lifetime blindly chasing ambition and becoming the person you think everyone else imagines you are, a weird thing happens. You eventually lose track of what it is you enjoy. I needed a new path for my life, and I wasn't sure where to begin. But starting in New York, I had been really dedicated to my diet, and lately had a passion for organic cooking. I would read anything I could find on health and nutrition and couldn't get enough information—so maybe that was my new path.

I kept it in mind but went about my daily life until one day I was scrolling Facebook and BAM! A targeted ad hit me like a ton of bricks. It was for an online school based in New York called the Institute for Integrative Nutrition, and it looked really interesting. This was the type of school that not only focused on mainstream health topics, but also on homeopathic healing, light and aroma therapy, and all kinds of natural-based health techniques. I decided to go for it.

For the next two years, I studied extensively about health, nutrition, and how to have better relationships. I learned about meditation, food, essential oils, illness, natural child birth, systemic inflammation, heart disease, cancer, the effects of magnesium and iodine, and numerous spiritual practices. I was devouring books and going to conferences, attending virtual classes and spending time deep in thought, and eventually, I came out with a degree as an Integrative Wellness and Lifestyle Coach. And by the time that happened, I had put it all to use in my own life.

The most interesting thing I found was a completely different way of thinking about health in general. Basically, the idea that food is actually secondary to optimal health.

I learned that there are really four major "food" groups: Career, Relationship, Physical Activity, and Spirituality. And if those four things are not clicking at a seven out of ten or better, nothing happens. It doesn't matter how well you eat—if those four areas are not in sync, you're not going to get healthy. It will be a never-ending uphill struggle because all of those things involve stress, and too much stress will prevent your body from functioning like it should.

People don't like this approach because they'd rather have a magic pill that makes everything better, but try it out. Pay attention to all four areas and see what happens. It's not rocket science.

For my part, I rated myself in all of those areas, and I felt like I had a pretty good grip on the first three. Career could be better, but I was working on that. Relationship was a solid nine because of Leslie. And for physical activity I gave myself a ten, because I loved to walk, bike, and swim. But for spirituality? That was an obvious zero.

I hadn't been to a church outside of wedding or funeral services since I was a boy and had written organized religion off as a bunch of hypocrites playing dress-up. Over the years I had felt that there was as unifying power in the universe, a creator of all this. But it was just a vague sense and I routinely laughed at the Christianity of my wife's family. I would tell anyone who listened that Jesus was a great healer and a great man, but he was only famous because he had a great PR firm, and the Bible was just a good history book.

Now I was finally open to the possibility that spirituality was indeed a real and necessary part of a healthy life, and it was in this setting that I showed up on stage at WME. It was here that I sat in to do a little expert panel for the Music Health Alliance. It was here that I accidentally spilled my guts about the trauma in my early life and how I had never confronted it in all my years. It was with this stuff rolling around in my mind that I finally began to think—maybe all this debauchery was my way of protecting myself from the pain I'd endured. It was here that I began to let love in—real love.

So I dug in deeper. But because of the opinions I had formed as a kid, I left Jesus Christ and the Bible out of my search completely.

My spiritual search started with the ideas that I was least familiar with. I guess I figured maybe there was something I had never been exposed to that would just start screaming, "This is it!"

I read books on gnosticism and its focus on personal spiritual knowledge, rather than church doctrine. I explored Buddhism and the quest to achieve enlightenment through suffering. And Hinduism was interesting, with its emphasis on things like honesty, self-restraint, good karma, and being one with the natural world. I started doing a lot of meditation and yoga. I even had several sessions with a local energy healer, but nothing really connected.

Now, had I not been such a prideful ass in my position on Christianity, I would have recognized the three amazing resources at my disposal—three people who would have been very excited to teach me about Jesus, the Bible, and being a Christian: my sister-in-law, Sharon, her husband, Don, and my wife's best friend, Angie, all of whom had accepted Jesus into their lives years earlier. But for the entirety of the twenty-four years I had known them, I was not at all interested in that exploration. They knew it and graciously gave me my space, but that began to change as my quest for health and spirituality progressed.

It was Christmas of 2014, and we were spending the holidays in Fairhope when it came time to exchange gifts. It was a small family gathering and the house was warm and fully decorated. We were all feeling the Christmas spirit I think, or at least drinking it.

The gifts were opened and we all smiled and sipped eggnog, and eventually, Don reached over and handed me two boxes. As I opened the wrappings, he said, "Every good Southern boy needs a gun and a Bible."

25

Bought The Farm

I had just received an intriguing gift, a two-part present that came out of nowhere and would have a profound impact on me: my first pistol since that awful night with Dockery so many decades ago and the New King James Bible. But I wasn't ready for what that meant just yet. When we got back to Nashville I put the Bible in a box in the storage closet, safely out of sight and out of mind and proceeded to the shooting range with my shiny new pistol. Lucky for me, my family had almost as much patience as God did.

But then 2015 rolled around, and Leslie and I were ready to do something we'd been saving up to do for years, and it would mark one of the final steps in my journey.

We were ready to buy some land. We wanted an investment for the future and also a spot to get away to our own little slice of heaven on earth. But little did we know, God had plans for the land too.

We started with lakefront property. That's what you do when you first start looking at investment property, right? It was beyond exciting. Nashville is virtually surrounded by good-sized lakes so there were plenty of options, both developed and undeveloped, but it wasn't exactly smooth sailing. We quickly realized there were drawbacks to being on the water, like drab winters and the fact that you pretty much need a dock and a boat . . . mostly so all your friends can come over to use your dock and your boat.

Then something came up for Leslie. One of her colleagues was selling a fifteen-acre farm they owned nearby, and Leslie offered to help find a buyer. Nashville was booming and we knew plenty of people moving to the city, but the more I thought about it, the more I wondered why we didn't look at it ourselves.

It wasn't on a lake, but our idea wasn't originally about being on a lake. It was to add land to our investment portfolio and to have a getaway we could escape to without traveling too far from town. A farm could accomplish that just as well as a lake house, maybe even better. Never mind that neither of us had ever done a lick of farm work.

I liked the idea and Leslie did too, especially since we were striking out with the stuff around the lakes. Still, we decided not to rush into anything and to take our search slow. And that lasted about two weeks.

With houses and real estate, I've always been able to feel if a place is right for us or not—it's about the energy and there's just a feeling I get. The first two farms we looked at did not speak to us at all. The third one, though, was like the Goldilocks of farms. It was just right with just the right energy.

It was situated outside of the little town of Portland, Tennessee, right up near the Kentucky border. That's a long haul from Nashville, almost an hour on a good day, but that wasn't necessarily a bad thing. We got in the car and headed up to look at it, and as we rounded a corner on a twisty two-lane road, my eyes traced a long gravel driveway that would change both of our lives.

To the right was a large, open pasture on a gentle hillside topped with a thick hedgerow. To the left sat a cute little brick cottage built into another hillside, back off the road just far enough to feel private and shaded by majestic old oak trees.

The main area was in full sunshine and had a small barn with room for some equipment and a few animals, plus lots of space for gardens. The property continued to slope gently away into a thick stand of old growth hardwoods. They looked like they probably went on for miles before hitting anything else.

A gentle breeze was blowing through the brightest red and orange leaves I had ever seen, and all around us acorns dropped to the ground as fall began to arrive. There was lots of potential to make the place our own—even an area off the side of the house to build a big deck for entertaining. And as we walked down the driveway, a pair of donkeys in the pasture brayed a loud hello.

I looked at Leslie and she looked at me, and without saying a word, we both seemed to agree this place was special. But it hit me especially hard. I felt my shoulders relax and my breathing deepen. It was like nothing I'd experienced before, and it still gets to me today.

On October 9, 2015, we officially became the owners of this beautiful forty-acre farm, a piece of land that had been owned by the same family since the mid 1800s. And right away God got to work putting our new land to use.

Having never farmed before, never driven a tractor or even tended a successful garden, I spent the next month going out every day to learn the ropes from the previous owner, Donnie, soaking up as much knowledge as I could before he moved to Florida. And every time I went out there, the energy of the land became more and more invigorating.

I would arrive early in the morning and have lunch underneath a shade tree as the birds chirped, then stay and work until the sun was setting over the trees. I vividly remember the last rays of a golden sunset filtering down through a tree full of even deeper golden leaves and feeling the most profound peace I had felt in many years. Within a week, I felt like the farm was where I wanted to spend all my time.

Maybe just getting out of the hustle and bustle of Nashville was the trick. It was fifty miles one way, but the more time I spent on the farm, the more I came to believe this purchase was meant to be. Even the street address felt like a sign from above—it was the same as the last four numbers of my cell phone number. The more time I spent there, the more I felt inspired to open my heart. But if we were brought here for a reason, what was the reason?

It all went hand in hand with the search for spirituality I had been on, which by now had led me to explore all the faiths I could think of except one. But by that Christmas, I was ready to hear the truth.

It was 2015, and Leslie and I were in Fairhope with Don and Sharon once again. For some reason I was feeling more optimistic about everything. Instead of focusing on the hypocrisy I had experienced in church as a boy, I was thinking about Jesus' message. A couple of months of life on the farm had already stripped away much of the anger and resentment I was harboring, and without that cynical armor, maybe I would see Jesus and his teaching in a different light.

I began to ask Don questions—about God, about the Bible, and about Jesus—and he was more than willing to teach. There were questions I had been holding since my childhood, and others formed during my time on the farm. Things like how a just God could allow wars of religion and disease? Why the poor are still poor and good people still get sick? How He could allow a kid like me to go through a loveless childhood, never having a father to look up to, and then leave me to try to be a father to my own children?

I finally gave Don the opportunity that he'd been patiently waiting for, and he spent the next four hours answering questions like that. He was teaching, not preaching, and it was like something broke free inside of me.

When we got back to Nashville, Sharon and Don suggested we listen to an online sermon from the church they attended, delivered by Brother Fred Wolfe. I hadn't been to a church service since the eighth grade, and quite frankly, still had no intentions to start again. But I was willing to listen.

Not knowing the subject matter or anything about it, we tuned in to the sermon on my phone as Leslie and I drove to the farm, and much to my surprise, it was all about the Bible as a book of history. Dang it, I thought. I was right all along, even this pastor thinks so. But Brother Fred was a fisher of men, and he was about to set his hook.

"Yes, the Bible is a great history book," Brother Fred said. "But pay closer attention. The Bible is HIS-story."

His-story? His-story? My mind was blown. This is the exact argument I had been using my whole life to brush the Bible off, and now here it was being turned upside down.

I made up my mind that if I truly meant to move forward with my spiritual discovery, I was going to have to investigate the Bible. When I got back to Nashville I dug out the one Don had given me the Christmas before. This was it, the moment I would finally find the missing piece of the puzzle. I was excited and beyond ready to be moved . . . and then nothing happened.

———————

I opened the Bible up and was immediately intimidated. The print was excruciatingly tiny. I only got about three verses in before I was lost. I had made a personal commitment to do this, though, and was deter-mined to find a way to connect with the Word. Luckily, modern tech-nology came to the rescue.

Instead of reading the actual text, I downloaded a Bible app to my phone. Whatever works, right? I dove in to a daily reading program and it was every bit as hard as I expected, but my determination began pay-ing off. I found other books to help. And whenever I got frustrated or didn't understand something, I would call Don to discuss. He had truly become my John the Baptist. An extraordinary teacher.

I felt totally armed and was now on a great path, reading like never be-fore with more questions than when I first started in radio and research-ing to the depth I had when I started nutritional school. From then on, I was at the farm almost every day, reading my Bible verses and trying to open my heart to God, hoping He would make Himself known to me. And although at first I felt like an outsider, like I was a stranger in God's house, I slowly began to feel more like I was welcome in the Gospels and welcome in Jesus' group of students.

Then I read through the Parable of the Prodigal Son in the Book of Luke, and was suddenly struck by the parallels in my life. It was un-canny.

Jesus tells this story to illustrate how unconditional God's love is. It be-gins with a man who has two sons—two sons who act very differently. After the man gives each son an inheritance, one of them stays on the farm and continues to live in quiet obedience to his father, while the other goes out into the world and quickly squanders his money, spend-ing it lavishly and selfishly until it's all gone.

But when he comes crawling back to his father, penniless and begging to be accepted as a servant, he's shocked when his father welcomes him with open arms. The prodigal son is not punished but celebrated for his return to the family (and to his senses), and when the man's other son asks why, his father explains.

"Son, you are always with me, and all that is mine is yours," he says. "It was fitting to celebrate and be glad, for this your brother was dead, and is alive; he was lost and is found.'"

Jesus means to show that God will always welcome his children back, and he'll even do so with a party. It's because being away from God is like being dead, and returning to Him is like being reborn. No matter how bad you've messed things up on your own, being reborn is worth celebrating.

It was like Jesus was speaking directly to me, and I was starting to really hear it for the first time.

26

The Awakening

We named the property Humble Hollow Farm after a prayer songwriter Lori McKenna wrote for her children (which country star Tim Mc-Graw turned into a Grammy winning hit, "Humble and Kind"), and I began to know I had been guided there by God. As the seasons shifted and I watched the land breathe in this cycle of growth, death, and re-birth, I could see His work plain as day.

I had come a long way in my spiritual walk, and at this point felt like I had found the right path. But as good as that felt—and it did feel great—I knew I still wasn't "there." I kept talking with Don, and over and over, I asked him, "When will it happen? When will I know that Christ has really come in to my life?"

I didn't know if I was going to be overwhelmed by a bright white light, or if I would spontaneously start doing cartwheels down the grocery aisle. Would I be struck to the ground? Or have a late-night visit from an angel? Will God reveal himself to me in the woods? Do I have to be in a church for this?

Again and again in a thousand ways I asked Don the same question, "How do you know when it happens?" And every time I asked, he smiled warmly and replied with a frustrating tip.

"Just listen," Don would say.

"Just listen?" That's not what I wanted to hear. I wanted answers right away, not a vague bumper-sticker slogan. But after hearing it a few times, those simple words started turning over in my mind. Suddenly it hit me in the heart.

How did I never think of this before? With a career built on my love of music, listening was a big part of what God had called me to do with my life. Discovering The Beatles and listening to John R on WLAC were the few things in my childhood I can truly say were positive. It's how I found joy for the first time. Listening to music made me feel less alone when I was just another fatherless kid, and it gave me purpose. It gave me a chance to turn out better than my dad did.

After all the turmoil of my life, God just wanted me to get back to the basics, to remember how to just be quiet and listen. It felt like He had spoken directly to me through Don, and even though I wanted desperately to keep moving forward, I took the advice to heart. I could be patient. After all, He waited patiently for me for sixty-some years.

So, I kept reading, praying, learning . . . and listening. I said prayers and read the Bible every day. I watched documentaries. I read other books and tuned into podcasts with spiritual thinkers. I was ready for God's love to consume me, but the waiting seemed to take forever. Many times I questioned what I was doing, but I always convinced myself to just listen. I had come so far and felt so close.

And when it finally happened, I understood what "just listen" meant.

———————

It was Thursday, October 10, 2017, and I was at home in Nashville preparing dinner for some friends coming over that evening. I had learned to love cooking over the years, and one of my favorite things to do was to start the food at about 1 p.m., and just take my time with some good wine and music.

As usual I was alone, and normally, when I cooked I would listen to something from my early childhood—The Beach Boys, Frank Sinatra, Sam & Dave, The Contours. Anything from the '60s was the usual bet, although I'm not sure why. Maybe it reminded me of something my mother would do.

But on this day, something strange hit me. From out of nowhere I felt the need to hear some contemporary Christian music, which was really odd because I had never been into it. I had heard a Christian song or two, but I knew absolutely nothing about the bands or what was going on in the Christian music scene.

I pulled up my music service and just picked a compilation, and right away, I was really digging the tunes. It took me back to my days of screening new music for the radio, and after a couple of songs went by, I was hooked. To me, each one sounded bigger and fuller than modern country or rock. The production was amazing. I liked it.

And then it happened. Alone in my kitchen, another song came on and I was enjoying this one too. But something was different. The lyrics were all about God's love, and how He wanted each one of us to know His love, even if we don't deserve it. It hit me HARD . . . like a heart attack right in my soul.

I lost all control of myself and was overtaken with an emotion I had never felt before, one I still struggle to describe. It was like a combination of every emotion ever, and it totally consumed me. I couldn't stand up, I couldn't grab the table. I fell to the floor like a weeping, quivering mess of a human, and all along this song just played on.

I could not stop crying. I was overcome with this intense feeling of a presence, something that gripped me like you would grab a wet dish rag and wring it out, and I was the rag. I wasn't sad, but I laid there and let myself sob, releasing a deep anguish that had been balled up inside my gut for . . . well . . . forever.

They were not tears of pain. I wasn't gripped by remorse for all I had done or sorrow for time lost. All of that seemed to lift up and out of my heart, and my tears were tears of the purest joy I have ever known.

I knew at that incredible moment that Jesus Christ and the Holy Spirit had filled my body, mind, heart, and soul. God had embraced me and welcomed me back like the father and his prodigal son. It was like the opposite of how I always felt during an angry blackout—instead of feeling nothing, I was feeling everything.

Finally I was strong enough to move, and I knelt at the kitchen counter, listening to this song over and over again, praying, asking for forgiveness, and thanking God for his loving mercy. Still in disbelief, I shook my head and thought to myself, Be still and know that He is God!

Somehow I finished up in the kitchen, and then went to my computer and wrote an email to Don sharing what had just taken place. I sent the email, but otherwise, I kept the news to myself. I didn't mention anything to Leslie or our guests at dinner. But once they left, Leslie noticed a different energy about me. I think I was still in shock.

I have never been able to hide my feelings from Leslie, and now I know that I have never been able to hide my heart from God. She asked me if I was okay. "You seem different," she said. So I shared my experience and we sat together and wept in grateful thanksgiving. She had shown me what love was all those years ago, and now I truly knew its source. I was saved.

The song that changed my life is called "Control (Somehow You Want Me)" by the band Tenth Avenue North, and it's like they wrote it for me and my journey, even today. It describes exactly where I was in that moment, searching for God but still unsure if He even wanted me. And that was nothing new. I had felt that way about the father figures in my life forever.

But the part that got me was something different—a moment where all that changed. With the sound of crashing drums, ringing guitars, and voices that reach up to the sky, I suddenly felt what God wanted me to know. That He does want me and that He's been calling out to me all my life. Even at my worst, He just wanted me to come home, so I did it. I gave over control, fully and completely, and went home.

———————

Don had told me to "just listen," and he was right—that's all I needed. It's funny because I was so worried about how it would happen, but I never imagined that music would be the thing that loosened the chains around my soul. I should have, though. It was my first love as a boy, and it's been with me all my life.

A little over a month later, Nashville was in the path of a total solar eclipse, and Don and Sharon decided to come up to Humble Hollow Farm to watch. What an amazing, God-filled event that was. For me, it was like watching His very hand reach out and prove to the world that He existed.

That evening Don and I were sitting on the deck, and as usual, deep in conversation. But this was a special occasion and we both laughed and shook our heads as we talked through my experience. It had really happened, and now we were bonded together forever. We even went through some more questions I had from my Bible studies, which I now had a different insight into. And after about an hour, I was once again overwhelmed by a presence that came out of nowhere.

Tears flooded my eyes and I felt that indescribable feeling from the kitchen a month earlier, like I couldn't control myself. God was moving me to say something, as if the time for listening had come and gone, and now I needed to speak. Don was still finishing a thought, but right in the middle of our conversation, with my eyes boiling over and a huge lump in my throat, I interrupted.

"Don, I need you to do something for me," I said. "I need you to baptize me."

He was moved, but said, "Why don't you wait until you come back to Fairhope, and let Brother Fred do it?"

"No," I replied. "I need you to baptize me right now."

So Don grabbed Sharon and Leslie as witnesses, and right there on our deck, in our hot tub, he baptized me. I gave my life over to Jesus Christ, my Lord and Savior.

27

Learning To Live

Since that day my life has been so very different, and accepting the love of Christ has been the most profound experience of my life. I've never felt anything like it—and I've definitely sampled my share of extraordinary feelings.

God's love goes way beyond any of that. After a lifetime of searching blindly for something to fill my soul and give me purpose, I feel complete. I even stopped drinking after fifty-five-plus years of daily use, and that alone is truly a miracle. From the time I was a teenager stealing from my mother's parties, I poured at least two or three and sometimes many more drinks every day, except for the two years while my liver healed, and now I don't even miss it.

I spend my days working the land or helping those willing to change their perspective get healthy, using a mix of God's Word and what I've learned about nutrition. And I don't feel so at war with myself or others. The constant cravings and impulses of my past are gone. I am at peace.

The farm remains my sanctuary and I continue to study the Bible daily, sticking with Don's advice and doing my best to listen for God's instruction through the Holy Spirit. But I've found that in order to truly listen, we sometimes need to block out the noise from outside. The noise that told me I was just an addict and wasn't worthy of true love. That I was just as bad as my father. And that's part of why this book was started.

I began this journey through my lifetime of sin and salvation for a reason—two reasons, really, and it wasn't just some sick form of boasting. First, I wanted to offer my witness statement that God can accomplish anything, even redeeming a man who spent sixty-five years doing everything He warns against.

I truly was the prodigal son of my own story, taking my gifts from God and squandering them at every turn, focusing on my own wants and desires and neglecting my duty to family—even lashing out with violence towards those I claimed to love. I polluted my body, and worst of all, denied God existed. And still, He took me back.

He allowed me to experience a true connection by bringing me and Leslie together, a revelation that pulled me out of my own head and exposed my heart for the first time. Then He removed me from the entertainment world I had wrongly used to measure my self-worth for so long. And finally, he showed me His love personally, revealing the basis for all human joy and filling a gap in my soul that had been there all my life.

But the second reason for this book was to see if I could figure out why I did what I did, to lead others to a better path.

Overall, I can see three main areas where I struggled—relationships, substance abuse, and ambition—and my problems with each of them go back to the same source. The way I looked at love was not as a support system based on giving, but as the physical act of sex and the question of what women could do for me. The way I handled my career was not as a means of providing for my family and achieving my full potential, but as a way to prove I was important. And the way I embraced drugs, thinking it proved I was in control and not afraid of anything—it was all about seeking acceptance from others and hiding from my pain.

I wanted to prove how good I was at my job, how talented I was, how cool I was, and how good I was in bed. I wanted everyone to like me, but looking back now, I don't think I even liked myself. And I've come to recognize this as the lesson God was teaching. He wants us to know we are all worthy of being loved.

It was an incredibly necessary lesson. I grew up in a loveless, faithless household with a mother who only cared for social status and had no compassion. She exemplified the idea that relationships were really just a transaction between two people possessing something the other wanted, and I was never taught how to love or even what love was.

I was just a teenager when I left home, and I had no understanding how to value myself, let alone others. I had no idea what life was all about (although if you had asked me, I would have been sure I did). And with no foundation to stand on, my relationships were all backwards, based on physical attraction and an unconscious desire for control over my lonely world.

I was searching for someone to show me love and make me feel worthy, but I never gave the love I was seeking back to anyone. And when this approach inevitably failed, I tried to cover it up with drugs and alcohol and more sex and constant work, lashing out with anger to deflect the blame and then trying the same thing again with someone else.

If I had only seen a loving bond between my mother and father, then perhaps I would have done things differently. Maybe I would have recognized God's love and accepted it early on, giving myself a sense of value that was just part of me, not created by my actions or station in life. Maybe I wouldn't have done so much damage to my own family.

In fact, I've read a lot about the special bond between a father and son since becoming a Christian. The Parable of the Prodigal Son is just one example where the Bible singles that relationship out.

After finding and accepting the love of my Holy Father, it made me more interested in the one I never had here on Earth, and I started seeking out information on my biological dad—which is something I never allowed myself to consider before, probably as a defense mechanism.

I won't put it mildly. What I've found has been shocking and eye-opening. Even though I never really met the man, we are almost the same person.

28

The Father I Never Knew

When I was a kid, my mother told me my father was a soldier who fought in World War II and Korea. But she didn't say much more than that. The only other things I knew were that my mother caught him cheating, so she left him, and that he'd gotten in trouble for writing bad checks and spousal abuse. As far as I knew, he was a deadbeat. But then as an adult, I did stumble on some evidence to the contrary. He'd won a Silver Star for gallantry in Germany, after all, so maybe I didn't have the whole story. I decided to dig deeper.

To my surprise, I came across a book titled Dachau 29 April 1945 – The Rainbow Liberation Memoirs, which recounted the horrifying tale of the American troops who stumbled into the Nazi's concentration camp at Dachau as World War II wound down. It laid out, in gruesome detail, what those men found and how they reacted, and my dad was featured in it pretty prominently. He was even quoted. This book held more information about my father than I had ever learned.

It turns out that Lt. Colonel Donald Downard was not some loser who got lucky in one battle and was cast off from the army for not being able to walk the line. He was a leader of men and a hero. The Silver Star was just the beginning, and at Dachau he played a significant role. But it would cost him.

According to the book, my father was the leader of 2nd Battalion, 222nd Regiment of the U.S. Army's 42nd Infantry Division (a unit known collectively as The Rainbow Division), and he was a seasoned combat veteran. He fought under the command of General George Patton and had seen some brutal action in Africa and Italy before reaching Germany. But when his unit moved into the camp at Dachau, they were stunned.

The cruelty of war had nothing on what the Nazis did to those people. Men, women, children, it made no difference. They were all treated as subhumans. But on the outskirts of the camp, sat a train, a silent, still hunk of metal that seemed oddly out of place. My dad had an experience there that must have scarred his soul forever.

It was April and the Bavarian spring was just beginning to bloom, creating this odd contrast of death, destruction, and barbed wire set over a colorful explosion of life with birds chirping in between ongoing rifle skirmishes. My father stood eyeing that train for quite a while. Eventually he took a detachment over to investigate and what they found seems obvious to us now. Back then, though, it would have challenged his notion of reality.

Car after car after car held a grisly cargo, a tangled pile of dead, skeletal-thin prisoners, thrown in like firewood until there was no room for more. The SS guards who murdered them didn't have time to dispose of all bodies they hastily created as the Allies advanced, so they planned to take them somewhere else. But they never got the chance. The Americans were enraged and disgusted with the scene, and my dad spoke of the experience for the book, although it must have been many years later.

"When we arrived at the camp, the first thing I saw was that terrible train," he said. "I walked past car after car. It was all I could do to believe it. Suddenly, a solider, about ten or fifteen yards behind me, yelled, 'Hey Colonel! Here's a live one!' Immediately, I ran back to the car. There, almost buried under a mass of dead bodies, was a hand that was waving so feebly you could hardly notice it. But it was moving!"

I can't imagine the horror of being buried alive in a pile of bodies like that, and neither can I imagine being my dad. As soon as he saw the hand, he climbed into the car and over those bodies, pulled that man out and started carrying him to an aid station. He didn't get one of the other men to do it, which the book notes as unusual. But there were still enemy units in the area, and the two men came under fire.

My dad was hit by a jeep as it rushed for cover and knocked unconscious, and when he woke up, he was in an aid station lying next to the prisoner he had just saved—the one and only survivor found in Dachau's infamous train of death. My dad went on to say his memories of that day were so terrible that he blocked most of them out. But something like that can't possibly be forgotten.

The reason I share this story is because I think I know how he felt and because of what I've learned of his personal life. Post-traumatic stress wasn't fully understood or appreciated back then, but he most certainly had it, and his life back home was messy and troubled in a way that had eerie parallels to mine. As it turns out, my brother and I were not the only children he had, or the only ones he walked out on.

After my parents' divorce, my father was married many more times—six times in total, just like me. He bounced erratically from one relationship to the next and had at least nine more children. And just like he did with me and David, he would cut his previous family off once he divorced their mother.

I know this because I've gotten in contact with one of his daughters—my half-sister—who, like me, knew little of our dad, let alone how many other families he had. She told me he was constantly working and had a terrible temper, was selfish with his actions, and had issues with drinking and domestic violence. And when he split with her mother, they never heard from him again. That last part cut me to the core. I did all of that too.

She was young when he left, just like I was when I left Jason, but the pain she carried was all too real. And even though he died in 1994, learning my father's story was almost like getting to finally meet him. I felt so strongly connected to him, and I clearly made many of the same mistakes. It was like someone describing another chapter of my own life.

It suddenly struck me that I'd spent my whole life hating my dad and trying hard not to be like him. But I might have had him all wrong. The trauma I experienced as a kid was real, and my dad's abandonment was a big part of that—I won't excuse him for it. It was the reason I struggled so much for so long. But he'd been traumatized as well. The war did something terrible to him. He was probably broken inside, just like me. So deep down, maybe he wasn't so bad. Maybe he was just doing the best he could, just like I was.

Slowly, through my faith in Christ, I began to forgive him. And through that, I was able to forgive myself for being like him. Then a realization hit me like a ton of bricks.

All along, I thought I was just another kid who didn't have a father, an emotional orphan who never learned to love. But in the end, I actually did have a Father. I wasn't alone. I just didn't realize it.

The love I never felt was waiting for me with God. He was there protecting me all through life, helping to shelter me and keep me going until I eventually found Leslie, and eventually Him. He finally got through to me that day on stage at WME and slowly led me home. It just took a long time to make the walk.

God's love is a parent's love. He said so as plain as day by sending us His son, Jesus Christ. He's always been my Father, through and through, and He loves me still today. Now I've found a way to fix the brokenness inside me forever. I just wish I had known it sooner.

29

Pay It Forward

When all is said and done, I know I was lucky. With everything I put myself through, I should have died long ago, by overdose or a drunk driving accident, or at the hands of some jilted husband. Like I said in the beginning of this story, I don't mean to boast about my past. But I'm not ashamed of it, either, and that's because of what I've learned.

I truly believe now that everything happens in God's time, and there is nothing we do that isn't God-driven. Leslie and I were meant to meet each other, and if not for some of the mistakes I made earlier in life, that may not have happened. I believe I was also meant to be on this farm, not only as the setting for my spiritual rebirth but as a place where God could lead me to examine my life and finally see what He has always wanted me to know.

I now recognize this one simple truth: God does not love what you have done or where you've been. He loves the person He created you to be. He loves the truth about you. He loves the purpose and potential you possess.

That's what a father does, and that's the biggest thing I've learned. A father steps in when things go wrong in a child's life, explains what happened and what that means for the future. He gives his children hope that the bad times don't define us. I have a fresh new perspective on that now, and I think it's my duty to share it.

I didn't have to drink myself to oblivion or turn into the Incredible Hulk when someone disappointed me. I didn't have to do cocaine until my nose nearly fell off or take risks trying to be a big shot in the music business. I didn't have to constantly chase sexual conquests or put my career above my kids. Those were all the actions of a man starving for love and acceptance, and we all know starving people will do desperate things. But God has a table that will satisfy that hunger. It's ready and waiting for each one of us, and I hope to get a few more guests seated.

I've started a ministry at the farm to do just that, designed as a safe place where men like me can come to heal their mind, body, and spirit—the concept at the core of the Tipping Point Artist Wellness program I've been slowly building these past years.

The ministry is called Bring It All to the Table, and it puts everything I've learned through my journey into practice. It's a long weekend of fellowship at Humble Hollow Farm where men who've struggled with faith can come and talk it out in a judgement-free zone while also communing with nature and nourishing their bodies with organic, locally sourced meals. The whole idea is for men to feel free to discuss real topics that may be too challenging for a church-organized group. I can understand where people like that are coming from, and I can help explain what life looks like from both sides of the coin.

Each time we do it, a handful of guests can bring their absolute worst to this table—all their fear, their sin, their burdens, and their past—and know they'll be hosted by someone who's been there. And by the end, they'll know without a doubt that their worries are nothing God hasn't seen before.

The idea was inspired by the unholy road I travelled in finding my way to God and the desire to pay the blessings I've found forward. After all, I tried everything I could think of to fill the emptiness inside me, but it was never enough. And that's because my hunger couldn't be satisfied at any old table. I had to give over control of my self-image and take a seat at my Father's table before I was finally made whole.

Now, I sit here at our farm, surrounded by the perfection of nature and that hunger is totally satisfied. It's like our own private Garden of Eden. I am not a powerful man or a famous one like I thought I wanted to be. I'm not a rich man either, at least in the sense of money in the bank. But I do have a huge stockpile of God's love, and that is more valuable.

He's in the vegetables we grow and share with our neighbors and in the braying of the donkeys when I walk out to the barn. He's in the sunshine that filters down through the rustling autumn leaves. But most of all He's in me. I feel His forgiveness and grace, and I know without a doubt it's what I've searched for all my years. I've even forgiven Jason.

It makes me think back to the kid I once was, sitting by the window with my radio each night. I'd spin the dial and search for a tune through the deep Southern static, imagining a life far away from where I was. Well, now that signal comes in loud and clear, and I know what I was really searching for.

I found the love I needed through a lifetime of music, winding and wild as it was, and once I did, my journey from cocaine to Christ was complete. But you might find God somewhere different, so keep your mind open. All it takes is to slow down, have faith, and believe. And then . . . just listen.

The Beginning

LANNY WEST
with Chris Parton

Lanny West is a music and entertainment industry veteran with more than six decades of colorful behind-the-scenes stories behind him. But after leaving the rock 'n' roll lifestyle behind, he's now turned the spotlight on Jesus Christ.

With a deep well of expertise in artist management, concert promotion, night-club operation, FM radio and more, West's high-flying professional career was matched only by a vibrant personal life filled with adventure ... and sometimes disaster.

In his in-depth memoir, *FATHER, SON & THE UNHOLY ROAD: The Dark, Twisted Truth of My Journey From Cocaine to Christ*, West shares the twisted tales which stitch that life together, leading to his born-again redemption and the creation of a unique men's ministry in Portland, Tennessee.

Careening through an era of tectonic social changes, West's career began in 1967 as a radio DJ in Western Georgia, rising up through the ranks as FM radio exploded in popularity. Over 11 years he pioneered new practices in the industry, culminating in the establishment of live programming for Y102-Montgomery and achieving #1 status in the market in only 10 months.

West continued to be involved with radio through 1979, while at the same time founding Lanny West Promotions – an independent record promotion company securing radio play for major recording labels across the region. His radio career also coincided with a concert-production tenure, which included large-scale shows for acts like ZZ Top, Pure Prairie League, Leon Russell, Molly Hatchet and more.

Throughout the 1980's, West made a name in the nightclub industry, where he started out as Music Programmer/Marketing Director for entertainment-and-hospitality giant, McFaddin Ventures. With that team, he helped launch and promote 28 nationally acclaimed nightclubs, before transitioning to UniHost in 1986 as the VP of Marketing and Entertainment. The move put West in charge of opening and operating Atlanta's infamous American Pie, which he helped build into nationally renowned entertainment destination with an A-list clientele.

By the early '90s, West had become the General Manager of *Hitmakers* magazine in Los Angeles, before returning to Atlanta as Vice President and Partner of

UniHost – charged with overseeing all aspects of the company's bar/restaurant operations, while spearheading new marketing, promotion and booking tactics.

West moved on to found JustWest Entertainment in 1995 and launch and/or manage the artistic careers of independent rock and folk acts like Matthew Perryman Jones, Becky Sharp, Sonia Leigh, 22 Brides, People Who Must, Memory Dean, John Faye, and more, before expanding in 2008 to the full service entertainment career strategy group, Tipping Point Entertainment Group, LLC. As Founder/CEO, West continues to manage the career of Senior Vice President of Music and Talent CMT, Leslie Fram, and offers personalized artist management and strategic consulting services.

West has also founded and run retail and restaurant establishments like the French Quarter Blues Cafe in Fairhope, Alabama, and LUXE and 1*FIVE*0 in Atlanta, Georgia, and he continues to serve as President of Fairhope's 4Bags fashion boutique.

But in 2017, everything changed. West experienced a powerful spiritual awakening after relocating to Portland, Tennessee, where he now resides on 40 acres of pristine farm and forest land. Moved to repair his neglected soul after decades of professional climbing, months of faith-tradition research resulted in a musically-charged rebirth through the grace of Jesus Christ. West was later baptized on the farm and now works to spread the Gospel to others, focusing on the unexpected freedom and peace found therein.

His book *FATHER, SON & THE UNHOLY ROAD: The Dark, Twisted Truth of My Journey From Cocaine to Christ* recounts the tale, and West now runs a growing men's ministry at his Humble Hollow Farm. Limited spots are available for quarterly, weekend-long "Bring It All to the Table" events, which aim to provide a judgement-free natural setting for men, couples and musicians to explore the issues that keep them from fully investing in their faith.

Christopher Parton is a Nashville-based editor and music journalist whose work has appeared in Rolling Stone Country, Nash Country Weekly, CMT, Nashville Scene, Nashville Lifestyles, Taste of Country and more. He is also the author of The Little Book of Country Music Wisdom.